THE CHILD AS A SENSE ORGAN

27. Nov. Basel : Lehrer —

1.) Geisteswissenschaft kann an den Menschen
heran kommen; naturwissenschaftl. Vorstellung
aber nicht.

2.) Vorstellen, Fühlen, Wollen verschiedene
Bewußtseins zustände.

3.) Mit den Entwickelungskräften wirken.

u.) Wollen — Nachahmung — Künstlerisch. —
Fühlen — Autorität — gedächtnismäßig.
Vorstellen — Urteil — Anschauung.

*Notebook entry by Rudolf Steiner
for a lecture on education in Basel, Nov. 27, 1919*

The Child

as a Sense Organ

*An Anthroposophic Understanding
of Imitation Processes*

Peter Selg

SteinerBooks | 2017

STEINERBOOKS
AN IMPRINT OF ANTHROPOSOPHIC PRESS, INC.
610 Main St., Great Barrington, MA 01230
www.steinerbooks.org

Translated by Catherine E. Creeger

This book was originally published in German as *Das Kind als Sinnes-Organ: Zum anthroposophischen Verständnis der Nachahmungsprozesse* (Verlag des Ita Wegman Instituts, Arlesheim, Switzerland, 2015).

Book design by Jens Jensen

Published with generous support from the
Waldorf Curriculum Fund

LIBRARY OF CONGRESS CONTROL NUMBER: 2017941249
ISBN: 978-1-62148-183-6 (paperback)
ISBN: 978-1-62148-184-3 (ebook)

Printed in the United States of America

Contents

"As unlikely and paradoxical as this may sound to modern ears, in the young child these forces derive predominately from the nerve-and-sense system. Because children's ability to observe and perceive is unconscious, one does not notice how intensely and deeply the impressions coming from the surroundings enter their organization—not so much by way of various specific senses as through the general 'sensory being' of the child. It is generally known that the formation of the brain and of the nerves is completed by the change of teeth. During the first seven years, children's nerve-and-sense organization, in its plasticity, could be likened to soft wax. During this time, not only do children receive the finest and most intimate impressions from the surroundings, but also, through the working of energy in the nerve-and-sense system, everything received unconsciously radiates and flows into the blood circulation, into the firmness and reliability of the breathing process, into the growth of the tissues, and into the formation of the muscles and skeleton. By means of the nerve-and-sense system, the body of children becomes like an imprint of the surroundings and, particularly, of the morality inherent in them."

Rudolf Steiner, 1923
(*Waldorf Education and Anthroposophy* 2, p. 68)

Preface

The most successful work by Swedish educational reformer Ellen Key, *Barnets Århundrade*, was first published in English as *The Century of the Child* in 1909. In general, the ideas expressed by Ellen Key were products of her time, imbued (sometimes with fatal consequences) with both the spirit of Darwinism and Key's exposure to Friedrich Nietzsche. Nonetheless, to historical hindsight, the book's title has had a certain validity and staying power. Owing to new insights in somatics, education, developmental psychology, and the social sciences and humanities, the early twentieth century saw an impressive upswing in awareness of the unique significance of childhood and of each child as an individual. In this catastrophic "age of extremes" (Hobsbawm), which brought disruption, separation, loss, and displacement to an extent never experienced or even dreamed of before, the most important topics of investigation included the significance of stable "bonding," or connection to a consistent "attachment figure."

As early as 1945/46, Viennese psychoanalyst René Árpád Spitz (the scion of a Hungarian–Jewish family that had emigrated first to Paris in 1932 and then to New York in 1939) published his initial research, "Hospitalism: An Inquiry into the Genesis of Psychiatric Conditions in Early Childhood" (1945), followed by "Hospitalism: A Follow-up Report."[1] These reports effectively placed the social connections of infants and toddlers and the importance of a central "attachment figure" in the center of his scientific work and, increasingly, of public discussion.

Spitz's studies, along with subsequent works by other researchers, revealed not only the importance of the processes of imitation and learning for children in the context of two-way relationships, but also the deficits—emotional and intellectual—that result when children are limited or "deprived" in this regard. Moreover, Spitz's early works demonstrated the essential importance of sensory stimulation and experience during the early stages of child development. He described the symptoms of hospitalism and depression, attributing them in part to "lack of stimuli" in "clinically sterile" medical institutions.[2] From the very beginning, he acknowledged that these problems were related to isolation—i.e., to separation from key attachment figures:

We do not believe that a *general* lack of perceptual stimuli is the key to deprivation syndromes [in children in foundling hospitals]. We believe they suffer because their perceptual world is devoid of human partners, because their isolation has cut them off from any and all individuals who might represent mother figures for children of this age. The consequence is a severe limitation of psychological capacity by the end of the first year of life.[3]

As early as World War II, the Scottish psychoanalyst James Robertson, along with his wife Joyce, became familiar with Anna Freud's work with hospitalized children in London, and they began exploring children's varying responses to separation. Shortly after the war's end, he began collaborating with and was urged on by John Bowlby and Mary Ainsworth at London's Tavistock Clinic, where he focused his investigations on hospitalized toddlers separated from their parents.

In 1952, with a primitive black-and-white camera, Robertson was the first to record the hospital stay of a two-year-old girl admitted for surgery, producing the devastating film, *A Two-year-old Goes to Hospital*. Like his other films, this groundbreaking exploration of issues such as continuity and stability of connections and quality of care for children is counted among the milestones of later "educational research."[4] The medium of film, which Robertson was using for purposes of research and documentation even before Spitz, continued to be developed and increasingly refined.

Beginning in the 1970s and '80s, such films (including, among others, those produced by Hanus and Mechtild Papoušek at the Max Planck Institute of Psychiatry in Munich) made it possible to microanalyze mother–child interactions, including the preverbal and bodily "dialogues" that develop on the basis of the child's imitative ability. These films revealed the reciprocity or mutuality of the activity, along with the many nuances and elements that recur repeatedly in the process of successful connection and stable binding and begin already in the first days and weeks of life after birth in the form of the finger games, playing with words and sounds, miming, and gesturing that are crucial to infantile learning and maturation. We learned that newborns—contrary to formerly undisputed assertions—are not only capable of seeing and hearing but also move in rhythm with their mother's voice in particular.

Later, at the University of Regensburg, educational researchers Karin and Klaus Grossman emphasized the significance of the mother's sensitivity for this process and introduced it into scientific discussion as a relevant factor in successful interaction and bonding.[5] Christian Rittelmeyer summed it up:

> In particular, more recent interaction analyses make it obvious that in the early years of life, incisive learning experiences for toddlers (and presumably also for slightly older children) are linked to the presence of a consistent caregiver who either already possesses these interactive competencies as identified through microanalysis or at least develops them in the course of caregiving.[6]

The caregiver's counterpart is the baby, with the capacity for spontaneous imitation, who establishes an "expressive resonance" from the very beginning of the relationship by responding with purposeful, non-reflexive movements to the caregiver's miming and repeated gestures (opening the mouth, sticking out the tongue, and so on). "At birth, infants are already capable of translating the miming they perceive into their own proprioceptive bodily sensation and corresponding movement."[7] "The newborn perceives the mother not as an opposite but rather mimetically by recreating her *gestalt* internally."[8]

Jean Piaget still assumed that in the weeks after birth (in the first stage of "sensory–motor intelligence"), infants exist in a state of "absolute egocentricity" in which they perceive only themselves. According to Piaget, all movements during this period are either simply spontaneous or reflex-like and only later become "random activity."[9] In the closing decades of the twentieth century, however, detailed interactional analyses clearly showed that infants seek human connection from birth and that sensory–motor development—including babys' increasingly comprehensive control of their own body—takes place through relationships, in playful, perceptible interaction (action and reaction) with the Other (primarily the mother). Thomas Fuchs wrote,

> In the recurring *gestalt* cycle of spontaneous movement and perceived response from the environment, infants adjust to their body and learn to control it. This process of sensory–motor familiarization, through which we actually "inhabit" the body, can also be described as "incarnation."[10]

At least in part, therefore, a successful "incarnation process"[11] is the expression of social experience, a dialogue that encompasses the infant's "own" body and leads (or contributes) to the baby's taking full possession of it. In multiple studies, Thomas Fuchs refers to phenomenological studies by the French philosopher Maurice Merleau-Ponty, pointing out that the human

body is designed for "intersubjectivity" from birth—
that is, even *before* language or self-awareness develops.
("The Other is already contained in the structures of
bodily experience, understood in expression and present as the object of desire."[12])

Here Fuchs refers to Merleau-Ponty's term *intercorporeal experience* (*intercorporéité*) as the domain
of shared bodily activity—the space of relationships,
where development occurs through processes of imitation in particular; Fuchs then demonstrates the importance of this space for understanding the processes of
interaction and communication that take place between
mother and child.[13] This means, however, that the phe-
nomenon investigated by Spitz, Robertson, Bowlby,
Ainsworth, Papoušek, Grossmann, and many others in psychology since the mid-twentieth century has
also become ever clearer in neurobiology (for example,
after the discovery of so-called mirror neurons in the
premotor cortex[14]).

According to cutting-edge science, we humans have
a greater capacity for imitation than any other species;
we are adapted to and dependent on it in the sphere
of social relationships. Infants experience their "attachment figure" not as a static "other" but "intercorporeal"
through a living dialogue, and grasps the attachment

figure's "intentionality," or inner orientation, to a certain extent, "reading" gestures and situations through an "implicit knowledge of relationship" (Daniel Stern) rather than through any process of assessment, of which the child is still incapable.

In this process, infants are markedly receptive, even organically transparent, to their surroundings. Internalizing experiences in the domain of relationships, babies not only imitate them, but also use them to continue to develop and penetrate their own bodily existence through the process Fuchs describes as "familiarization," or more to the point, "incarnation." ("Newborns perceive the mother not as an image or Other but *mimetically* by integrating her movement *gestalt* into their own."[15]) Throughout this process, babies are extremely susceptible to stimuli. In other words, their bodily organization literally depends on what they experience—or do not experience, as the case may be—from outside.

Beginning in the final two decades of the twentieth century, "neuroplasticity" research demonstrated that the human central nervous system adapts both functionally and structurally to stimuli—i.e., to sensory experiences that either promote or inhibit development and become deeply inscribed on the child's physical state (specifically, the central nervous system).

As research continues, the infantile brain, long seen as a genetically predetermined blueprint guiding the "equipping" of the individual, is increasingly revealing its true character as an organ whose postnatal development (in terms of the numbers of neurons and linkages among them, growth of synapses, and complexity of associations) depends on the quality of its experiential environment. This development benefits from varied stimuli (through movement, impressions of color, and experiencing language and music) and is damaged both functionally and structurally by factors such as sensory deprivation, media overload, and traumatic experiences.

> That the crucial shaping of central nervous structures takes place only in the course of ontogenesis and in constant interaction with the environment is a key finding of recent brain research. The discovery of neuronal plasticity proves the circular relationship among brain, body, and environment: Our experience of the world structures our central nervous system just as much as the structure of the CNS shapes our experience.[16]

It has also been shown that the corresponding changes, although occurring primarily in the central nervous system, are by no means limited to it; their consequences extend to *the body's organization as a whole*.

(In 1997, for example, Montgomery et al. published an exemplary study of 6,574 children, showing a connection between the experience of family conflicts and reductions in growth.[17])

In his fundamental monograph, *Das Gehirn als Beziehungsorgan* (The brain as relationship organ), Thomas Fuchs merged a multiplicity of findings and results into a phenomenological–anthropological view of the interconnectedness of the brain, the organism as a whole, and the social (interactional–dialogic) environment and transcended the reductionism of the scientific discipline of neurobiology to describe human experiences as embedded in an overarching "ecology."

≈

"What works from one individual to another is really much deeper than we ordinarily suspect."[18] The foregoing—very brief—overview of the secular research can form a backdrop for the synopsis of Rudolf Steiner's definition of imitation and its significance for anthroposophic developmental physiology and education as presented in this book. It will then soon become evident—if it was not already—that Steiner's richly comprehensive and differentiated presentations on this topic were not pursuing some "romantic," antiquated theme.

Rather, he was dealing with a complex of questions that further development has shown to be among the most important chapters in the anthropology of relationships and "incarnation." They are exceptionally relevant not only to education and psychology but also to medicine.

> The child's feeling, empathetic experience of what is going on in the surroundings generates organizing forces that penetrate all the way to the blood vessels. We must picture the scope and extent of this phenomenon to distinguish truly between what is inherited and what is acquired from the environment through imitation during the first period of the child's life. Then we will recognize the marvelous interaction between the child and the environment, and we will be able to place the actual scientific concept of heredity (a seemingly mystical concept for level-headed observers) on a totally different foundation.[19]

When Steiner made these statements in a lecture in Prague (April 39, 1923), they might have still sounded far-fetched, "theosophical," or "occult" to his audience. Now that seven decades of research into relationships, bonding, interaction, and neuroplasticity have intervened, however, the verdict cannot remain the same. On the contrary, Steiner's statements *anticipated* the course of these directions in science after the mid-twentieth century. As he emphasized in Stuttgart on June 1, 1924, "Much of what is now attributed to murky, mystical 'heredity' should actually be sought in the child's natural tendency to imitate, which is perfectly straightforward." He went on to point out that, for the most part, the importance of experiencing dialogue and interaction is still underestimated, while the genetic dimension is hugely overrated.[20] *"The sensory-nervous system remains waxlike in its plasticity for the first seven years of life."*

Rudolf Steiner never wrote a monograph on the anthroposophical anthropology of perceptual and imitative processes in children, nor did he ever devote a single lecture to that topic alone. Instead, he returned to it repeatedly in a great variety of contexts, usually in his educational presentations to teachers and parents, in which he spoke of the need for a new art of education based on Spiritual Science. He emphasized repeatedly that one of the key challenges facing the future of education was to develop a "new anthropology" that would involve "consciously acquiring insight into the human being."[21] He described anthroposophical anthropology as a requirement of the times, emphasizing that a new educational ethics or "attitude" could not simply be acquired as such and taught in universities or teachers' colleges, but would become possible only on the basis of an authentic relationship to knowledge (*Erkenntnisbeziehung*)—i.e., a "living relationship to the emerging human nature in the child," which requires a deeper understanding.[22] What teachers urgently need, he said, is a new "direction in thought," in the sense of a "new anthropology." In his lecture series during the founding of the first Waldorf school in Stuttgart (1919), he said,

> The main difference, the thing that is most effective in teaching, is the line of thinking teachers bring through the door with them. Teachers who actively entertain thoughts about human development have a much different effect on their students than do teachers who know nothing about all that and never give it a thought.[23]

≈

It would certainly be worthwhile to consider the details of Rudolf Steiner's perspectives on the process of sensory perception, imitation, and relational and bodily development in children, as presented in subsequent chapters in conjunction with the most recent findings of modern developmental psychology and developmental physiology, including neurobiology. This present small volume, however (along with earlier studies in anthroposophic developmental physiology and pedagogy already published by the Ita Wegman Institute[24]), is more limited in its purpose, which is simply to compile Rudolf Steiner's extensive treatments of the topic from many different lectures on Spiritual Science and to reveal the conceptual connections among them.

The next step, then, would be to relate Steiner's spiritual-scientific depictions to the findings of empirical sensory research, with their mutual elucidation as the goal. In my view, however, if that step is to avoid either apologizing for or trivializing Steiner's contributions, it must take place on the basis of a discriminating disclosure such as I am attempting here. In principle, it is conceivable that those who are not anthroposophists will someday, too, take an interest in efforts to bring sensory–empirical, phenomenological, philosophical anthropology, and spiritual-scientific anthropology[25] together. In the case of the topic discussed here, those non-anthroposophists would be progressive scientists who are at home with research on issues and problems in child development (including imitation, empathy, and neuroplasticity) and who become aware of Rudolf Steiner's treatment of the subject for purely objective, inherently topic-related reasons, without philosophical bias or fear of compromising their academic positions.

≈

This book is published in conjunction with the "Endangered Childhood" conference of the Anthroposophical Society in Switzerland, exploring the hazards and risks and the helpful forces to which the incarnation process is exposed during the first seven years of life. A little more than one hundred years ago, seven-and-a-half months after the outbreak of World War I, Rudolf Steiner spoke these words in Nuremberg on March 13, 1915:

> Those who feel called upon to contribute to sustaining the souls of our children and children's children in the face of what will befall humanity in the twentieth century need to realize that their contribution will have to be a strong, inner, spiritual force. To an extent far greater than we can already imagine in ordinary life today, our twentieth-century successors will need powerful soul-sustaining forces if they are to carry humanity's spiritual wealth, accumulated over the course of centuries, into the future. The descendants of today's earthly humanity will be exposed to completely different upheavals in their lives.[26]

Peter Selg
Ita Wegman Institute
Arlesheim, September 2015

The Incarnation Process
in the First Seven Years

*Above all, understanding the human being
involves the insight that the developing individual is subject to developmental stages to a much
greater extent than we ordinarily assume.*[27]

*The child is a completely different being before
and after secondary dentition.*[28]

In his lectures, Rudolf Steiner repeatedly sketched the
challenges and difficulties that incarnation presents
in the early stages of an earthly biography. The child (or
rather, the spirit–soul of the reincarnating individuality)
is coming from a totally different sphere that, though
related to the earthly world, has as little or nothing in
common with it. Rudolf Steiner spoke of conception
and embryonic and fetal development and, especially,
postnatal development as states of being displaced into

"a completely different world."[29] "We are accustomed to the spiritual substance from which we drew spirit-life before descending to Earth. We are accustomed to dealing with this spirit substance," which, in a certain sense, "we prepared ourselves."[30] But this spiritual substance in the sphere of the unborn must be left behind when we enter the earthly world and begin the transformation into a (developing) bodily being—a process that Steiner once described, in drastic terms, as "martyrdom." ("What martyrdom the spirit undergoes initially when descending into an infant body!"[31]), even if the child does not experience it consciously. "The child has to enter a world that is often not a good fit. It is a terrible tragedy to undergo this process consciously."[32]

The first period of childhood is essentially about adapting to this situation, establishing a provisional balance between the "spiritual" and the "physical," between the prenatal cosmic and the earthly factors. In the fall of 1919, in his preparatory course for the future teachers of the Stuttgart Waldorf School, Rudolf Steiner outlined several fundamental steps in maturation against this general anthropological background, describing "proper breathing" and "proper sleeping," as key aspects in developing (i.e., actively acquiring) equilibrium in the incarnation process. About "learning

to breathe" under the circumstances of postnatal existence, Steiner said,

> Out of all of the human being's connections to
> the outer world, breathing is the most important.
> But we begin to breathe only when we enter the
> physical world. In the womb, breathing is still
> an interim type of respiration that does not yet
> establish a full connection to the outer world. In
> the true sense, breathing begins only upon leaving
> the womb, and it means a very great deal to the
> human individual.[33]

According to Steiner, breathing is the most important "mediator" between the human individuality
entering the physical world and the new, earthly "outer
world," to which an actual connection must now be
developed. Steiner pointed out that, although healthy
newborns are already capable of inhalation and exha-
lation, it takes much longer (into the first few school
years) to develop the actual connection between rhyth-
mic respiratory processes as the bearers of emotional
experiences and the sensory–nervous processes that
are so extremely important for sense perception and
conceptualization. Developing this connection provides an important, even indispensable, impulse for the

incarnation process—that is, for the entry of the soul-spiritual element into physical, bodily nature.

> The human being entering physical existence has not yet created the right harmony, the right balance, between respiration and sensory–neural activity. The child has not yet learned to breathe in a way that supports the neurosensory process appropriately. As a result, the most important educational measures involve observing everything that supports the integration of respiration into neurosensory activity in the right way. In a higher sense, the child's spirit must learn how to take in what is received through being born in order to breathe. You see, this aspect of education fosters an inclination toward the spirit–soul element: *By bringing respiration into harmony with neurosensory activity, we draw the spirit–soul element into the child's physical life.*[34]

Rudolf Steiner added that it is similarly important to support the acquisition of rhythm in sleeping and waking. Contrary to popular opinion, this involves more than simply developing regular sleep habits. Once again, there is also a close physiological connection to the child's overall organization. Although children are born with the ability to "sleep," "they are not yet able to carry what they experience on the physical plane into the spiritual world, where they can process it and bring the results back with them to the physical plane. Young children's sleep differs from adult sleep in characteristic ways."[35] From the spiritual perspective, for the human being on Earth, both inhaling–exhaling and waking–sleeping are gestures of incarnation–excarnation. Both of these fundamental processes, says Steiner, have to do with merging "the living body and the soul-spirit or spirit–soul"—that is, with intermingling and harmonizing the physical world's life processes (and thus also its *experiences*) with the soul–spiritual way of life that characterized the child before birth. ("Initially, therefore, all instructional and educational activity is directed toward a very high plane, toward teaching proper breathing and the proper rhythm in the alternation between sleeping and waking."[36]) Neurosensory processes are of special or even central importance in mastering the interplay or successful integration of "the living body and the soul-spirit or spirit–soul."

≈

In principle, as Rudolf Steiner emphasized repeatedly, development during the first seven years of life is markedly dependent on the "head system," which is its central instrument or organ in all respects. As Steiner once put it very succinctly: "What (or who) actually carries our "I" when we descend from the spiritual world into the physical world through birth? The head is the carrier of the "I," the vehicle that transports the "I" into the physical world."[37] In presenting this topic, Rudolf Steiner often stressed the stark contrast between the (relative) stillness of the head system and the child's movement-filled prenatal environment:

> As paradoxical as it may seem to superficial observers, we are actually in constant motion in the spiritual world before we start preparing to be born here on Earth. Before birth, we dwell in the element of movement, but if this movement were to continue, we would never be able to enter the physical world.[38]

The stillness of the head system "safeguards" a child against remaining in the all-pervasive mobility of life in the prenatal or preconception state. Once the "I" has "ridden" into the body, its "vehicle" comes to a standstill.

> Even when the rest of the organism is moving, the head remains uninvolved. Once the "I"—which was in constant motion before birth—descends into the physical world, it holds still, like a person sitting motionless in a moving carriage or train. It is no longer in motion as it was before birth.[39]

All subsequent development then proceeds from the head, which remains (relatively) still. ("During the first period of life, the child's development proceeds from the head."[40]) The stimulus for further development comes from the head system—that is, from the individuality active within the "vehicle" of the head. "The force of the child's individuality works from the head outward."[41]

Steiner continued, saying that, from the physiological-anthropological perspective, the work of development during the first seven-year period (in the overall context of learning "proper breathing" and "proper sleeping") consists primarily of detailed refinements to the body's functional and morphological organization as a whole, concretely guided by the head system and the forces at work within it. In this process, the power of the child's individuality works *through the head,* like a "spiritual sculptor."[42]

> Inwardly, the child shaping his or her own organism is an amazing sculptor, an outstanding sculptor. No sculptor is able to create world forms out of the cosmos as wonderfully as a child shaping the brain and the rest of the organism during the time between birth and the second dentition. In fact, the child is a marvelous sculptor; the sculptural energy is simply

working within the organs as the internal force of growth and development.[43]

From the head, the organizing forces *"radiate"* throughout the body:

> Consider the child. Actually, all of the sculptural, formative forces proceed from the head. The sculptural, organizing forces that shape the growing organs appropriately radiate from the head into the rest of the organism. What proceeds from the head consists entirely of sculptural, formative energy.[44]

This process takes place simultaneously with the development of the head system itself—that is, in conjunction with the ongoing development of the central nervous system after birth:

> The *most extensive activity of these forces is applied to sculpting and organizing the brain,* but it also extends down into the rest of the organism, shaping and organizing, intervening directly in the human being's substantial or material aspect, triggering material processes.[45]

The sculptural, organizing process that proceeds from the brain pervades the organism in all its individual aspects and depths, extending even into the material processes of physical existence. According to Steiner's later accounts, this molding activity takes place largely through air and warmth processes in which the force of the child's "individuality," or "spirit–soul" (the "I" and the "soul body"), are concretely at work.[46] These air and warmth processes are governed by the central nervous system and work in the craniocaudal direction (from head to foot) to permeate the living body— i.e., the physical and ether bodies[47] "radiating from the head into the child's physical body and ether body, right down to the toes and fingertips."[48] "The human head is the great sculptor who shapes the blood vessels and activates circulation and so on."[49] "Until the second dentition, the child's blood formation depends on the head system."[50]

In many passages in his lectures, Steiner uses the short form "head" or "head system" to denote the impulse-giving center of child development in the first seven years of life. From the overall context of his presentations and the passages already cited, however, it is clear that he was talking primarily about the head-centered neurosensory system, or the brain: "As strange and paradoxical as it may sound to modern ears, all the forces of a child's organization emanate *from the neurosensory system.*"[51]

Contrary to outer appearances, "brain activity," says Steiner, is "the most active" in children, concretely "radiating" the "sculptural organization of the entire body."[52] These "rays" or "streams" originate in the neurosensory system.[53] In some individual lectures, Rudolf Steiner described an "inner layer" of the central nervous system within the head system as the "sculptural apparatus most heavily involved in this process"[54] and emphasized its "developmental" activity.[55] Although these statements were probably either difficult or impossible for most of Steiner's listeners to understand, he persisted in using them, returning to them repeatedly if only briefly, and was clearly counting on future scientific work, including conventional scientific research into human physiology and anthropology, for further details. Speaking to medical doctors, he said:

> All organs take shape from the neurosensory system. If you want to confirm this empirically, begin with the senses that are localized in the skin and spread out throughout it, such as the senses of warmth and touch, and try to visualize how the overall form of the human organism has been sculpted and developed through these senses, whereas the forms of specific organs are shaped by other senses.[56]

This process of organization and development is related to the fact that neurosensory activity is not clearly localized or even systemically or functionally defined during early childhood. Instead, it "resonates" throughout the body, as Steiner repeatedly asserted:

> We must be aware that, in the small child (under age seven, more or less), neurosensory activity, the rhythmic activity of breathing and circulation, the activity of movement, and metabolic activity all intermingle everywhere, but in such a way that neurosensory activity dominates. In children, respiratory and circulatory rhythms and metabolic activity are processes that we cannot understand in their true nature unless we see neurosensory activity *continuing to resonate* in them. When a child sees a face furrowed by cares, the initial effect is that of a sense impression. That impression, however, crosses over into how the child breathes and from there into the musculoskeletal and metabolic systems.[57]

> It is not simply that children receive the subtlest impressions directly from their surroundings. *Through the intervention of the neurosensory system on the energetic level,* everything they observe and perceive flows into their blood circulation as a whole into the consolidating

respiratory system, into tissue growth and musculoskeletal development.[58]

The effects of neurosensory processes extend to the body's "outermost periphery,"[59] where they are of crucial importance, both functionally and structurally, right down into bone formation and hardening. The illnesses typical of the first seven years are also dependent on and determined by the "resonance" and dominance of neurosensory processes throughout the organism:

> All of the characteristic childhood diseases actually originate in the head and spread downward through the rest of the organism as a result of a certain *overstimulation of the neurosensory system*. This is the case even in pediatric cases of measles and scarlet fever. In how childhood diseases manifest, we can see that they are primarily reactions to states of excitation in the neurosensory system. We need to know this to reach a true pathology of childhood diseases.[60]

≈

On the other hand, Rudolf Steiner made it clear on numerous occasions that the effect of neurosensory processes on the organism as a whole must not be understood simplistically or one-sidedly. Rather, we must consider the fact that the other bodily functions and maturation processes also work back on the head's neurosensory system and support its further development. Children integrate themselves into their surroundings through the experiences of learning to walk and talk, which are then reflected or inscribed in the neurosensory system. In this context, Rudolf Steiner spoke of the *"embodiment of the 'I,'"* which takes place through processes such as walking and talking that then work back onto the body and the nervous system. With regard to the processes associated with developing uprightness and learning to walk in the first two years of life, he said:

> When we observe a child's growth from a tender age to the second dentition, we see how an internal factor increasingly comes to the surface of the organism. We know that these are the years when the head in particular is undergoing development. Anyone who traces this development, unconstrained by what current science tells us, will be able to observe a stream running through the human being *from below upward.*
>
> While the child is learning to walk—outgrowing the helpless state of not being fully able to walk and needing to lie down or be carried—what is stirring in this part of the human body,

the limb person, emerges as a revelation of will impulses that are expressed in more than just outward wriggling or, later, being able to stand up and walk. These impulses work back on the entire human organism. Today's science is already somewhat aware of these things—they are there for the taking in physiological research—but is not pursuing the right path. In the future, when we actually study the head as it is transformed during the progression from the helpless state to standing on one's own legs to using them for walking, we will discover how what emerges in the limb person is then reflected, so to speak, in the parts of the brain that constitute the will system. Indeed, we must say that when children learn to walk, they are also developing the brain's will system, working out of the peripherally located limbs and from below upward.[61]

In another lecture, Rudolf Steiner warned against naïvely placing excessive emphasis and value on the neurosensory system (the "neuronal person," as he called it.) It is not completely true that the brain directs the body; rather, it interacts with it in a two-way relationship and in connection with the environment. In spite of his own marked emphasis on neurosensory processes in early childhood development, he called it a "false anthropology" to overemphasize neuronal activity, saying,

First of all, we give the nervous system credit for far too much, while understating the importance of the stream flowing through the entire human body from below upward. Limb activity, along with everything we do in relation to our environment, is reflected in the nervous system—specifically in the brain. Thus we must not see it as contradictory when the anthroposophical view of the human being tells us that encouraging children to make the right movements at an early age fosters the subsequent development of their intelligence, discernment, reason, and common sense. When we are forced to wonder why a certain child makes poor decisions or demonstrates confused judgment at age thirteen or fourteen, the answer often lies in the fact that appropriate hand and foot movement was not encouraged in early childhood.[62]

In this same context, talking about speech acquisition and how it works back on the neurosensory system, Rudolf Steiner said,

Continuing to trace the individual's development, we see that the next important phase is experienced by reinforcing and individualizing the respiratory system, just as the limb system acquires a more individual constitution through walking. And this transformation and reinforcement of respiration, which is physiologically traceable, is then expressed through everything we acquire as a result of speaking. Once again, there is a flow through the human organism from below upward. What is incorporated into the neuronal system through speaking is traceable; we can see increased inwardness of feeling radiating from within when a child learns to speak. Through learning to walk, we insert ourselves into our neuronal system. Similarly, through learning to speak, we find our way into feeling. *These are interesting connections that will need ever more study.*[63]

This is how the "embodiment of the 'I,'" the penetration of the body by the power of the child's individuality, takes place—not merely from head to foot, but also in the opposite direction, by experiencing the world and the effects of its forces as a consequence of actually starting to feel at home in one's surroundings, which is also a "settling in" process of adapting to earthly circumstances, laws, and forces. ("We unite with certain earthly forces by orienting the body to them. We learn to stand upright and walk; we learn to insert ourselves into the balance of earthly forces with our arms and hands."[64])

In addition to the detailed features of the brain's structure and functioning, said Steiner, even the child's physiognomy continues to develop and unfold as a result of these experiences. ("Every day, every week, every month, the child's non-specific facial features gradually become more defined, just as the newborn's clumsy movements gradually become more coordinated as the child grows increasingly at home in his surroundings."[65]) By degrees, the child's "physiognomy gradually rises to the body's surface from deep within" as the child increasingly gains control over his body.

According to Steiner, however, what we are seeing here is "essentially the embodiment of the 'I.'"[66] The child's spirit–soul aspect works "from below upward," "drawing (although initially unconsciously) from the surroundings whatever it needs to incorporate into that most material of aspects, the head system, in the form of thinking, feeling, and willing."[67] Steiner then elaborated, saying more precisely, "The aspects of our environment that we experience *through imitative activity* in learning to walk, speak, and think are imprinted" on the brain and neural system. With reference to physical anthropology as a whole, Steiner continued,

> Everything superficial physical psychology tells us is true: The brain is a clear imprint of what the person is on the soul level. We must know, however, that the brain does not *create* the soul. Rather, it is the foundation on which the soul

develops. Just as I cannot walk without solid ground under my feet, as an earthly human being of course I also cannot think without a brain. But the brain is nothing other than the basis on which thinking and speaking configure what we bring from the world around us, as opposed to inherited predispositions.[68]

It is simply not the case that children develop their specificity and personalities on the basis of a "genetic matrix" of inherited intellectual and other "endowments" (along with a few "environmental influences"). Rather, the unconscious "I," or force of individuality, works its way into the surrounding world, where, by coexisting with objects and actively experiencing that world, forces developed or initiated *through the "I"* then work back on the developing brain. This activity is part of the incarnation process, the "embodying of the "I," which is both a "horizontal" and a "vertical" process, in that it is facilitated and influenced by the social context in which it takes place.

≈

Steiner tells us that the activity of the "physical principle," which encompasses a process of consolidation and concentration that leads to but is not identical with the consolidation of the skeletal system, is of central importance in the first seven-year developmental period and in the child's developing organism. The child's spirit–soul aspect is coming from a dynamic prenatal, preconception world of "movement," a spherical world of expansiveness and "dispersion." In contrast, the individuality's arrival on Earth and unavoidable incorporation into the world of earthly forces seems like "martyrdom."[69]

In this connection, Rudolf Steiner described the onset of secondary dentition (marked by the eruption of the second set of incisors around age six) as the "noteworthy end of early childhood" and of the process of "growing into the [earthly] outer world."[70] According to Steiner, the development of the first set of teeth (the primary teeth) is bound up with the forces of the past in the head,[71] and that of the permanent teeth (which have larger, harder, and more characteristically shaped crowns) to forces that "shoot into the head from the rest of the organism"[72]—i.e., forces that develop, or materialize, in relationship to the environment.

The second dentition and its feat of "crystallization" marks the "final thrust" of the principle of concentration, consolidation, densification, and even hardening that is so essential during the first seven years.[73] Thus the onset of secondary dentition also expresses the fact that the years-long dominance of the neurosensory system has been overcome, or at least largely balanced out, by increasingly strong forces emanating from the lower organism and its active involvement with its surroundings. Steiner spoke of the ongoing development of the sympathy-imbued "blood principle," which offers increasingly robust opposition to the (antipathetic, distanced) "nerve principle"[74] and marks the transition to the second seven-year period of development and to school readiness.

In this context, Steiner also described the second set of teeth as much more closely associated with children's individuality than the first,[75] saying that their development should be seen in connection with the ongoing individualization of the entire body. In one of his educational lectures, he emphasized that the secondary dentition "is only the outer expression of the replacement of the old body *with a new one*, which the soul–spiritual aspect works on [throughout the first seven-year period]."[76] The child's parents and the sequence of generations into which the individuality incarnates provide a "body template" of sorts that forms the basis for developing an individualized body after birth and over the course of many years. In a longer explanation, Steiner puts it like this:

If we observe very carefully and precisely just how different the second teeth are from the first, what happens to the person between birth and secondary dentition becomes almost tangible. From birth to the change of teeth, the entire human body is like a template of sorts. The forces of heredity prevail in the physical aspect, and the spirit–soul aspect, as a purely imitative being, works on that template according to impressions received from the surroundings.

Consider a child's relationship to the surrounding world—how the child observes every soul-stirring in its entirety and senses the spirit aspect behind the adult's every hand gesture, glance, and facial expression. These sense impressions then ripple throughout the child's body. When we observe all this, we note that, over the course of the first seven years of life, a different body develops on the basis of the template provided by heredity. As earthly human beings, we are each given a template provided by hereditary forces, and on that basis we develop the second body that is actually "born" when secondary dentition occurs. That the baby teeth are being ejected from the body by their replacements is a sign that some aspect of the person's individuality is pushing its way through the body and throwing off the trappings of heredity. The same is true of the human organism as a whole. During the first seven years, it was the template-like result of earthly forces. It is discarded just as we discard our body's peripheral outgrowths by cutting our fingernails, hair, and so on. Like the outer aspect that is constantly being cast off, the entire human body is renewed when the permanent teeth erupt. But this second body, which completely replaces the first one supplied by physical heredity, takes shape under the influence of the forces we bring with us from pre-earthly life. Thus in the period between birth and secondary dentition, the forces of heredity, which belong to humanity's physical stream of development, do battle with the forces that the individuality of each single human being brings down from pre-earthly life as the consequence of individual earlier lives on Earth.[77]

According to Steiner, the second body is generated with the help of experiences acquired from the environment, which then become jointly formative or transformative: "The spirit–soul aspect, as a purely imitative being, works on that template according to impressions received from the surroundings." The force of the child's individuality, however, is ultimately what is addressed by and active in experiencing the environment, and as such it is crucial to the entire process. That force, though lacking self-awareness, imprints itself on the bodily aspect as it is developed and transformed.

Thus the child's "I"-organization, or force of individuality, attempts to leave the "hereditary body"—and in fact the entire realm of heredity—behind, although without complete success. Sometimes, the old body, instead of being simply a template to transform, is followed slavishly, whether out of weakness or through unconscious choice.

> Heredity, in the sense intended by modern science, applies only to the person's first seven years. After that, anything "inherited" is actually a matter of free choice or simply following the model. In actuality, the hereditary aspect is discarded along with the first body with secondary dentition.[78]

The intention—even if not fully accomplished—is to "completely transform the entire human being.[79] Because secondary dentition is apparent to our sense of sight, we are especially aware of it, but it is only an especially "radical" expression of this process.[80]

~

Rudolf Steiner goes on to tell us that, during the first seven years, the child's body-shaping or body-transforming forces are essentially etheric in character and are applied to the physical body. But as the second physical body completes its development and becomes functional, these forces are freed up, step by step, and become available for more soul-oriented activity. Steiner repeatedly emphasized the transformation in the child's being that is marked by secondary dentition at the end of the first seven-year period. He describes this transformation as based on this fact:

> In the seventh year, forces that were previously forces of organic development—impulses that formerly worked in the breath, in blood circulation, in the overall development of the organism, in growth and nutrition—now leave only remnants of themselves behind to serve organic activity and transform themselves into the child's metamorphosed soul activity.[81]

Elsewhere Steiner said:

> What radiates from the head into the child's entire physical body and ether body, radiating right down into the tips of the fingers and toes, is the same as what later works within the soul in the form of reason and memory. The only difference is that, after the permanent teeth erupt, the child begins to think and memories become more conscious. This whole change in the child's soul life indicates that certain forces that become active as soul forces after the seventh year had been at work in the living body prior to that time. The

entire period of growth prior to the second dentition is a product of the same forces that manifest
as forces of reason or intellect after the seventh
year of life.

Here you have an actual interaction between
soul and body in that the soul emancipates itself
from the body after seven years and becomes
active on its own rather than within the body.
With the seventh year, these forces now emerge
and become active as soul forces, and they serve
that function into the next incarnation. During
this transition, what streams upward from the
body is repulsed, and the forces that shoot downward from the head are also intercepted.

The period when the baby teeth are being
replaced is a time of the most intense struggle
between downward and upward-striving forces.
Secondary dentition is the physical expression of
the struggle between the forces that later become
forces of reason and intellect and the forces that
will later need to be applied to drawing, painting,
and writing. All of the upwardly directed forces
are put to use when writing is developed out of
drawing, because these forces actually want to
transition into sculptural activity, drawing, and
so forth. They are the sculptural forces that once
shaped the child's body, coming to a conclusion in
the second dentition. We take advantage of them
later when we guide the child toward drawing,

painting, and so on. For the most part, these are forces implanted in the child by the spiritual world, prior to conception. *They work first as body forces that shape the head, and then, from the seventh year onward, as soul forces.*[82]

The state of existence preceding the metamorphosis at the end of the first seven years is unique. In this same context, Rudolf Steiner repeatedly described it as "lack of separation"—that is, a state in which "organic and soul activity" are united.[83] "[At this stage,] the entire soul–spirit aspect works in such a way that it actually consists of physical, bodily processes. Similarly, all physical, bodily processes are simultaneously soul and spirit processes."[84]

The release of the sculptural, formative forces from the body and subsequent metamorphosis does not happen abruptly but is an ongoing process that proceeds from above downward.[85] The result is the gradual emergence of "independent" soul activity that is not directly bound up with organic processes. In this context, Rudolf Steiner talked about the emancipation of the child's forces of intelligence from the physical body,[86] which he considered one of the most decisive criteria for school readiness at the end of the first seven-year period.

We see how the forces now developing in the child mean that the child has become capable of generating ideas independently. The capacity for independent ideas, which to some extent free a child's inner aspect from the environment, is not present at all before the seventh year. In connection with secondary dentition, the child gains a certain inwardness and then gradually becomes receptive to abstract ideas.[87]

Steiner also once wrote that *imitation* belongs to the period of the physical body's development during the first seven years, just as *meaning* speaks to the child's etheric body after secondary dentition.[88] During the transition period, the modality of the child's memory, initially body-related to a great extent, also changes from a "more physical–bodily experience," which becomes habitual and skilled through the process of imitation, to an experience that originates in spirit and soul.[89]

But how did Rudolf Steiner understand the imitation process itself, which is of preeminent significance for the first seven years?

2
The Imitation Process:
"Like an Eye that Touches"

According to Rudolf Steiner, the child working through the head system and the power of individuality—more than just the "sculptor" shaping the rest of the body—is *"all sense organ and all sculptor."*[90] This means, however, that the nervous system can sculpt and organize effectively only to the extent that it is connected to the sensory system. The *neurosensory* system, therefore, is what possesses the aforementioned "sculptural dynamic"[91] with regard to the body's organization as a whole.

Thus Steiner directed attention to the special character of the senses in childhood, particularly in the first few years of life. Through their senses, children are fully exposed to (and to some extent at the mercy of) objects and people around them. *"In a certain sense, the child is 'all sense organ' and confronts the world as such."*[92] In many of his lectures, especially those dealing with education and developmental physiology, Rudolf Steiner emphasized that the anthropology of early childhood must not only recognize the child as a "comprehensive" or "universal" sense organ, but must also give that recognition top priority in any consideration of what is involved in the child's life and experiences. "Children are completely like sense organs in how they take in the contents of their surroundings."[93]

Approaching the surrounding world with profound, even fundamental, forces of sympathy,[94] children unite their entire organization with the resulting perceptions, "submerging" into their surroundings[95] less through any individual sense than through generalized susceptibility to sense impressions. In other words, children are completely sense-oriented, completely receptive to sensory input. The individual sense-organ fields of activity are broader in children than in adults, and Rudolf Steiner saw this as contributing to children's "generalized sensibility" and their uniquely sensory orientation. Using the sense of taste as an example, he emphasized repeatedly that children tend to taste with the entire digestive system, not merely within the concentrated area available to adults.

The child tastes with the stomach and is still tast-
ing even when the nutritious fluid is absorbed into
the lymph vessels and passes into the whole body.
The child at the mother's breast is completely
infused with taste, so to speak, illumined, and
irradiated by taste. Later in life, that soul experience is no longer spread out throughout the body
but is limited to the head.[96]

"In the child, taste is sensed at a much greater depth in
the organism; the organ of taste, as it were, extends
throughout much of the body."[97] For example, the
"intense sweetness" of breast milk" "pervades" the
child's entire organism.[98] The child is "entirely taste-
perception"[99] and dwells in the unity of soul and organic
existence (i.e., experiences life forces that have not yet
been transformed into forces of consciousness). Further:

As with the sense of taste, so, too, with the other
senses. In the child, light's influences unite with
respiratory rhythms and submerge into blood
circulation. What adults experience as isolated
in the eye, children experience throughout the
entire body.[100]

This means not only that the fields of activity of
individual senses are more extensive than they will be
later, but also that the child's entire bodily existence is

sense-like in character: "In a certain respect, the whole body relates to the outer world the way the senses do."[101]

As Rudolf Steiner says elsewhere, the child's whole body is "like an eye that touches."[102] What is perceived and taken in by this "eye that touches" or "generalized sensibility" is internalized—that is, united with the child's own existence right down into the depths of the body—with an intensity that will never again be achieved by older children, adolescents, and adults:

> When I breathe in oxygen from the air around me, I immediately transform that part of the outer world into my own inner world, into part of what works, lives, and weaves within me. Similarly, as a seven-year-old, along with every soul breath I incorporate whatever I observe in a gesture, facial expression, action, word, or even (in a certain sense) a thought coming from my surroundings into my own being. Just as oxygen from the environment pulses on in my lungs, in my respiratory and circulatory apparatus, so, too, events in my surroundings pulse on within the little child.[103]

Neither the nearly unbounded connection of a child's body and soul to the surroundings nor the open and, in some respects, exposed character of the child's existence allows for any distance.

During the first period of earthly life—and the tendency persists until the incisive turning point in the relationship of the "I" to the world in mid-childhood[104]—sense impressions are not yet "reflected" in the mirror of consciousness, not yet judged and assessed (and thus separated to a certain extent from the child's organic existence), but go on working in the life processes of physical embodiment.

> At this point the child is not yet able to perceive, judge, and have feelings about sense impressions. It is all one; the child perceives; that perception is simultaneously also judgment; and that judgment is feeling and will impulse. It is all one. The child is completely inserted into the flow of life and has not yet broken free of it.[105]

In spite of the sometimes-unequivocal tone of his lectures, Rudolf Steiner had no interest in making absolute statements, since he was well aware that children's capacity for consciousness is always developing and increasing. In particular, children born into modern industrial societies of the twentieth and twenty-first centuries may present markedly precocious intellectual achievements and other defining elements of distancing. Steiner pointed out, however, that the forced and accelerated phenomena of speech-related conscious activity so massively fostered by our civilization should not obscure the fact that, even now as before, children who are developing healthily remain unconsciously inserted into the "flow of life"—that is, they actively follow events in their surroundings, internalizing them as described above. Only around the beginning of the second seven-year period are they in a position to recall remembered experiences at will and to manipulate concrete mental images freely.[106]

Moreover, the anthropology of early childhood shows that, despite all the many intervening influences, the capacity for empathy and imitation remains one of this period's most significant characteristics. Rudolf Steiner sometimes described the child as a "soul sense organ" and children's devotion to the surrounding world as downright "bodily–religious"[107] or "sensory–pious"[108] in character. Explaining the one such passage in an educational lecture, he said:

> In the period up to the onset of secondary denti-
> tion, when children are imitating everything, all
> of their sensory, physical behavior strives to be
> imbued and enlivened with feelings that will later
> find expression only in religious devotion or par-
> ticipation in rituals. Of course this phenomenon
> is especially strong in early childhood and gradu-
> ally declines with age; still, it does persist to some

degree until the second dentition. When human beings enter physical life, the body is awash in religious needs. The love that comes later is a weakened form of this actual religious feeling of devotion. We might say that, prior to the emergence of the permanent teeth, children are essentially imitative beings, and "bodily religion" is the form of experience pervading this imitation as their very lifeblood. I hope you will not misconstrue this expression. To describe something effectively that is so foreign to our modern culture, it may be necessary to use strange-sounding expressions, hence, "bodily religion." Until the second set of teeth emerges, a child lives in a state of bodily religion.[109]

Elsewhere, Steiner said:

The important point here is that in adult religious activity, the spirit–soul is completely absorbed in the world's spiritual aspect. The religious relationship is one of active submission, of beseeching mercy in submission to the world. In the case of adults, the submission is to a spiritual element; soul and spirit submit to and merge into their surroundings. It may seem that we are turning this relationship on its head when we talk about the submission of the child's *body* to its environment as a religious experience, but in fact this is an actual experience of natural religion. Children submit to their surroundings, dwelling in the outer world like eyes that separate from the rest of the body's organization and submit to their surroundings in devotion, beseeching mercy. This is a religious relationship shifted downward into the natural world. If we seek a sensory image for what happens on the spirit–soul level in adult religious experience, we need only look at the child's body before the onset of secondary dentition. The child dwells in religious experience, but that religion is the religion of nature. In this case it is not the soul that experiences submission to something greater, but rather the child's processes of blood circulation, respiration, and nutrition that "pray" to the surroundings.[110]

Together with the little child's receptive, world-exposed, world-imitating mode of being, "bodily religiousness"—that sense-oriented "prayerful" relationship to the world based on profound, even elemental, forces of trust and sympathy—accounts not only for the extraordinary capacity for learning typical of childhood, but also for the risks it entails. More than simply applying any means whatsoever in attempting to change little children's fundamental approach to life or to take away their unbiased power of devotion through premature cognitive development, our modern civilization—characterized by (if not actually obsessed with) intellect and technology—will exploit this fundamental anthropological relationship as long as it still persists, specifically targeting it with advertising and consumption strategies. Rudolf Steiner tells us that children tend to lose themselves in their sense-perceptible surroundings: "As the eye loses itself in the outer world of color and light, so, too, children lose themselves in the outer world."[111] Further, "[Children] want to be just like what they see around them."[112] They have an essential constitutional receptivity to manipulation of almost any sort, however, and are largely helpless to defend themselves against it. Their desire to be "just like what they see around them"[113] can be selectively targeted and exploited for economic purposes.

Moreover, sensory stimuli and environmental configurations profoundly influence the constitutional development of both body *and* soul in ways children cannot escape. In no later developmental periods can we be shaped from outside to the extent possible in the "plastic" period of childhood, when (as Rudolf Steiner put it), the "sensory element penetrates much deeper into the interior" than is later the case:[114] "In the child, psychological stimulation of every sort merges into circulation, respiration, and digestion. Body, soul, and spirit are still a unity, and consequently any stimulus produced by the environment extends into the child's bodily nature."[115] In the first seven years of childhood, approximately,

> the neurosensory system is the primary player in the organism as a whole, and all impressions of the outer world work throughout the organism, whereas later in life their physical effects are limited to the periphery of the sensory system and they work into the body only on the soul level.[116]

Moreover, as Steiner describes elsewhere, during the first seven years any forces from the lower organism are insufficient to counteract these sculptural neurosensory forces or to dissolve impressions that, once received, always tend to "take on form within the human body."[117]

The "dissolution" of the aspect of sense impressions that otherwise tends to "consolidate" is mediated by the blood principle, begins already within the sense organ itself, and gains strength and significance *after* secondary dentition sets in. ("Events taking place in the choroid of the eye are already attempting to dissolve any consolidation in the optic nerve. The optic nerve is constantly attempting to create contoured structures in the eye, which the choroid and the blood flowing in it then constantly attempt to dissolve."[118]) Until the end of the first seven-year period, the child is largely at the mercy of "indissoluble" perceptions and their organic consequences.

It is important to realize, however, that Rudolf Steiner did not consider childhood sensory impressions simply as submissively suffered impressions of a "foreign environment" and children as their passive "victims." Rather, he spoke of children's active will-involvement in approaching, perceiving, and internalizing the world. He saw this active will as at work already in the sensory system in children, which he characterized as the domain of "feeling willing."[119]

As he described in detail, the will nature in children extends into sensory perception. In one lecture, Steiner even summed up the makeup of a child's bodily existence and relationship to the surroundings as a "will-sense organ,"[120] "a sense organ in which the will is active in all of life's steps."[121] To a greater extent than is the case with adolescent or adult sensory activity, children's sense organs are still jointly defined by the will-related element of the blood, which is the vehicle for sympathy and is also characteristic of the sensory realm in animals.[122] In this same context, Steiner also said that children's impressive capacity for focused attention is often mistakenly credited to (neuronally mediated) conceptual activity—"We often allow ourselves to be blinded by that"[123]—whereas children are actually guided first and foremost by their body-oriented will and "pay attention" in that sense. The *will attribute* in children is what is inclined "to merge totally with the surroundings."[124]

The child's intense will is at work not only in perceptual activity in relationship to the surroundings but also in the (similarly self-activated) process of internalizing them—that is, in the aspect of perceptions that takes on "a unique inner form of experience."[125] "Consider the first stage in a child's life. Observed without bias, a child of this age appears not only as an imitative being *but also as a will-being*."[126] "When the eye takes in the outer world, will power working through the organic instrument is applied to the construction of an inner image of the impression, which then works into organic nature. Similarly, through imitation originating within, children constantly attempt to reproduce what is present in their surroundings."[127] Children are exceedingly active in the process of "repeating" absorbed perceptions, "imitating" them creatively. Imitation emerges *deliberately* from the child's "inner being" as the expression of independent activity.

As Steiner put it in Basel on November 27, 1919, the "lines of force" and "rays of force" in the child's will are modeled exactly after events in the surroundings.[128] His somewhat more detailed discussions of these processes in other lectures included the statement that the child recreates and "sculpturally incorporates" visual and acoustic impressions. He called this process the essence, what we generally know as imitation: "In the act of sculpturally incorporating what is seen and heard, the child is totally an imitative being."[129] This "sculptural incorporation" originates in the child's urge toward an "inner gesture"—i.e., in the desire to re-experience a perception from the earthly, sensory world in full inwardness, and thus the need to recreate it.[130] According to Rudolf Steiner, this process sets in already on the etheric level in the sense organ itself but does not remain restricted to it: "In every sense organ, the will-like element creates the inner image."[131] Like sense perception itself in childhood, the activity of imitation encompasses the child's entire bodily nature.

≈

Children are able to "give shape to their own developing forces through instinctive imitation."[132] Imitation "entices" the internal organs to assume their "form,"[133] said Rudolf Steiner in one lecture. In a notebook he wrote, "Children *imitate*—that is, shape the body according to what they see."[134] Through completely unconscious imitation and "experimentation,"[135] children learn to organize the body in ways that allow them to incorporate into and participate in the world. All of the aforementioned processes of "embodying the 'I'" via the deliberate activities of standing upright, walking, and speaking (and their impact on the development of the head's neurosensory system) have to do with these processes of imitation.

"Practice leads to skill," said Johannes Tauler in his Christmas sermon.[136] Rudolf Steiner explained that, in the little child, the capacity for recollection and memory has not yet assumed the character of mental images; rather, it is a bodily or "implicit" memory (Fuchs[137]) associated with "habitual" soul behaviors. The little child's body continues to develop through life experiences and the inward activity of imitation. Experiences, rather than being consciously reflected, distanced, "objectively" viewed, and "remembered," are "internalized" and united with the child's own being in a body that stores them and carries them into the future in the form of dispositions. Explaining the different types of "memory" in children during and after the first seven years of life, Rudolf Steiner said:

> For a child in the first period of life (that is, before the onset of secondary dentition), "remembering" is a habit, or skill, of sorts. We know that once we have slowly mastered a skill such as writing, we do it largely out of a certain flexibility that the physical organization has acquired through learning. If you observe a child tackling some activity, you can see how the term *habit* applies. We can see how that person discovered the appropriate limb movements for the job, which have now become a habit or a skill. Right down into the subtlest aspects of the child's organization, "skill" develops as the soul's response to what the child has done through imitation. Today, tomorrow, and the next day, the child imitates—not only with regard to outer bodily activities, but also in the body's inmost depths of being. This process leads to a type of memory that is unlike the memory that develops later, after the second dentition, when the spirit–soul aspect separates or emancipates itself from the body, as I mentioned earlier. The result is the development of a non-bodily image, an image of soul experience, within the human body. That image emerges again and again whenever we approach the same situation or the event repeats or there is some

inner inducement to call up the image. In young children, memories do not yet evoke images. After the second dentition, concepts or images that have been experienced reappear, but before the second dentition we dwell in habits that are not internalized as images. (Bern 1924)[138]

In an essay published three quarters of a century later (in 2000), Thomas Fuchs wrote:

Body memory, therefore, is the foundation of our living *being,* not of our self-*knowledge*. We might say that we *own* our past in the act of remembering, whereas we *are* our past in all aspects of bodily life.[139]

3

The "Other"
as Active Opposite Counterpart

The comprehensive connection of little children to the surrounding world involves almost all sensory modalities, but Rudolf Steiner stated that the single most important factor in a child's being and becoming (as well as with regard to the internalized and imitated "world") is other human being—the child's most active and effective relationships. During the first seven years of life, children have a *"total physical sense of the other person,"* Steiner emphasized.[140]

Those with whom children live—their companions and attachment figures—are the most decisive factor in their environment. As Steiner emphasized in his first course of lectures for future teachers of the Stuttgart Waldorf School, "The child's spirit–soul element, the sleeping spirit and dreaming soul, is still external, still outside the head, but it dwells among the people in the child's surroundings."[141] Children perceive, internalize, and imitate many different impressions, whether constructive and helpful or damaging. Most, however, are conveyed by people in the immediate surroundings who are actively connected to the child. They reveal the world to the child; initially and throughout the early years, they *are* the world. They represent it, reveal it, and allow the child to experience and incorporate it. Their importance, the personified power of their presence, and their authority (which means not only their soul–spiritual forces, charisma, and affection, but also their physical nature) are all implicit in Rudolf Steiner's striking statement that children "have a total physical sense of the other person."[142] That other person, the child's counterpart in a genuine, essential relationship, is experienced and imitated comprehensively.

A relationship to the non-human kingdoms of nature is also preeminently important for the configuration and development of children's experiential world and their organization as body–soul–spirit. Nothing or no one, however, is as essential as the very first relationship. In itself, that other person's perceptible existence already constitutes a totality, a true "cosmos," while at the same time being the child's bridge to everything else.

In the child's experience, however, this "other" or counterpart is a "mobile," non-static being. According to Rudolf Steiner, children remain related to movement, actively seeking it out and absorbing it, because they enter earthly life from a dynamic prenatal world of easy, shifting mobility and constant change. As the head system continues to develop after birth, its tranquility creates a point of support, giving the unfolding "force of individuality" a toehold in the earthly world and providing the prerequisite for individualizing the body's structure on the basis of internalized perceptions.

In the outer world, however, the child's soul remains related to movement—to sensory "activity in the surroundings,"[143] as Rudolf Steiner never tired of emphasizing. It is not so much the attachment figure's uniqueness of being that a child perceives, internalizes, and imitates; rather, it is the intentional movement of that person's form. The child is most urgently interested in "images of events, of actions in the surroundings"[144]—*gestures,* in the broadest sense of the word, through which the individuality of the Other manifests and is expressed and actualized, revealing its life. The child's "natural religious" connection to the surroundings relates to "gestures" more intensely and effectively than to anything else: "The physical body makes it

46

impossible for the child to avoid surrendering to *every-thing gesture-like*."[145]

Rudolf Steiner continued, saying that relationships involving movement and "meaningful gestures," rather than the accomplished facts of adults' actions, are most accessible to the child:

> The child does not yet have any capacity for per-ceiving human actions. Rather, what the child perceives in the surroundings consists entirely of meaningful gestures. In the first stage of life, we are actually involved in understanding meaning-ful gestures, and those meaningful gestures are what the child imitates.[146]

Thus, what impresses the child is not any "moral action" on the part of adult attachment figures. That is neglected, overlooked, or not experienced as such at all. Rather, the child takes in the much smaller elements of movement—facial expressions, posture, hand move-ments, whole-body movements—that are the "gestures" of embodied life, as Rudolf Steiner pointed out repeatedly:

> In particular, what is extracted from impres-sions of people in the surroundings—whether we move slowly or boisterously in the child's presence, revealing a spirit–soul attitude of non-chalance or vehemence, respectively—all this is

taken in by the child with an intensity almost equivalent to the intensity with which sense organs take in impressions.[147]

According to Rudolf Steiner, these "gestural" movements, which are transformed into "images of events or actions in the surroundings" in the child, also include the other person's speech—*not* finished statements (the counterpart of fully formed "actions," which the child does not perceive at all) but rather the movements of speech itself, the development, articulation, and ensoulment of individual sounds. The child dwells in and imitates these movements long before grasping their "meaning."

Children learn to speak because they can hear, because they can listen to what the sense of sound can perceive. Speaking itself, then, is mere imitation. Thus, you will also find that children always imitate speech sounds long before they understand any sort of concepts. If you observe closely, you will see the truth in this—a sense for sounds develops first, followed by the sense for meaning. Thus the sense of sound is the possibility of perceiving not just arbitrary sounds but also what we call speech sounds.[148]

Imitation penetrates deeply into the human physical and soul organization.

We must realize that the vibration or wave pattern of any spoken sound is sensed with much greater intensity in childhood than later in life. Each subtle adjustment of the larynx and the whole process of inwardly ensouling the [speech] organs is based on speech—on speech and imitation, when we are dealing with the mother tongue.[149]

Rudolf Steiner offered many comprehensive discussions of walking, speaking, and thinking—the three steps central to developmental physiology and psychology.[150] In one particular presentation, he placed special emphasis on the process of imitation:

As the human being matures into the physical world, inner development initially proceeds from gestures and *movement relationships*. Inside the organism, *speech* develops through relationships among movements and *thinking* then develops out of speech. This connection is like a profoundly significant law underlying human development. All that emerges in speech sounds results from gestures transmitted by the interior of the human organism. If you are attentive to how children who are learning to speak are also mastering walking, you will be able to observe how one child places more weight on the heel while another tends to walk on tiptoes. You will see how some children tend to stick their legs out in front of them while others hang on to something between steps. Watching children learning to walk is tremendously interesting and something we must learn to observe.

Even more interesting (and far less frequently considered) is how children learn to grasp and make hand movements. Some children move their fingers when they reach for something; others hold their fingers still. Some extend their hands and arms while the upper body holds still; others immediately follow up on the movement of the arm and hand by moving the torso. I once met a very small child who would "row" toward the table, moving his whole body, when his highchair was placed some distance away and he wanted to reach some food on the table. He could not move his arms and hands at all without setting his whole body in motion.

This is the first thing we need to look at in children, because how a child moves reflects the initial inmost stirring of life. Within this movement, the tendency to adapt to other people's gestures also appears immediately—to make movements like those of Father, Mother, or other family members. The principle of imitation emerges in gestures. Gesturing always appears first in human development and is then transformed inwardly into the unique structure and functioning of the individual's body, soul, and spirit, as well as into speech. Those who can observe this process in children know that heel-walkers invariably speak in choppy sentences, toe-walkers in run-on sentences. Children who tend to emphasize vowels use only their fingers for grasping, while those who emphasize consonants involve the entire arm to a greater extent. How a child speaks gives us an exact impression of his or her predispositions.

Then, in turn, the ability to understand the world, to grasp its meaning through thoughts, develops out of speech. Thoughts do not engender speech; speech engenders thoughts. As human culture developed, that happened with humankind as a whole? Humans spoke first, and then began to think. The same is true of the individual child, who *learns to speak, to articulate by moving; only then does thinking emerge from speech.*[151]

Children take all of these developmental steps, however, in a social context, in relationship to other human beings—that is, among attachment figures who are gesturing, moving, speaking, and thinking— through a process Steiner calls "comprehensive perception of the most intimate sort."[152] The important point here is the *inner content* of what is perceived, the active soul–spiritual element the child grasps unconsciously along with the other person's movements and articulation. According to Steiner, children's sense experiences are all more content-rich and deeply rooted than "outer appearances" would indicate, especially with regard to perceptions of their fellow human beings, who not only move through space and express themselves through speech but also always do so as beings of spirit and soul incarnated in physical bodies. In his pedagogical lectures Steiner said:

> As human beings, we are the outer imprint of our thoughts to a much greater extent than we realize. Although how we move a hand is a faithful impression of the sum total of our soul constitution, our inner tuning, it receives little attention in daily life. As adults exercising our developed soul activity, we pay little attention to the connections between our leg movements, hand gestures, or facial expressions and the impulses of will and sensing that reside in the soul. Children, however, do react and adapt to these imponderable aspects of life."[153]

A person who is moral and truthful has movements, facial expressions, and a way of walking that are different from someone who is untruthful. These differences in outer appearances completely elude us as adults, whereas they are real and present for children. Children do not become aware of the morality of those around them through mere conceptual activity or intellectual knowledge; rather, when they see people's movements, they discover what to imitate through a deep-seated subconscious understanding of mysterious indications inherent in how people express themselves.[154]

The details of self-expression that adults hold back in their souls—thoughts that remain unspoken, manifesting only in a subtle play of facial expressions or in faster or slower movements prompted by those thoughts—persist and continue in children's souls. We will be astonished to discover the extent to which children meld not only with the physical but also with the soul and spirit revelations of their surroundings.[155]

"From morning till evening, I was as good as alone in their midst. All help, all offers of a hand when in need, all teaching they received, came straight from me. My hand lay in their hands, my eyes rested on their eyes," wrote Johann Heinrich Pestalozzi about his life with the war-traumatized children of Stans.[156] In 1799, he applied his pedagogical intuition to attempting to support and educate those children and succeeded beyond all expectation.

In the first seven years of life—in their constitutional sensory capacity as "eyes that touch"—children perceive the morality of the other moving, acting, expressive people within their perceptual field. Occasionally a child's intuitive grasp of a moral situation is then articulated quite directly, to the astonishment of those around them. Much more frequently, however, it all remains hidden, even from the child's consciousness. Moreover, relatively few of the perceptions that children accumulate are dramatic or "expressive."

Although Rudolf Steiner certainly did not underestimate the significance of major events and traumas in children's lives, his many lectures attempted to draw attention to the supposed "banality" of "everyday," which consists of hundreds of "gestures" and speech movements in the child's immediate surroundings and countless small individual elements that are nonetheless crucially important. He did not construe the "moral illumination" of the world through the child's "universal sense organ"[157] as an actual value judgment, but rather as the child's imitative participation in the other person's soul world, which expresses itself in "gestures" and is grasped by the child in the "implicit knowledge of relationship" (Stern), as well as internalized through perception. ("Inwardly, therefore, the child is completely permeated with a father's irascibility, a mother's love, and whatever comes from anyone else. All of this extends right into the child's physical body."[158])

≋

Children relate to the other person's overall being from the very beginning, especially with regard to people in their immediate surroundings, and enter an active inner connection in which they perceive and imitate that total being and the other person's individual manifestations of life. The connection itself, however, is always essential in this process, as well as with regard to prioritizing whom to imitate. ("Sympathy for the being that the child chooses to imitate—sympathy that emerges "between the lines" of life, if I may put it like that—is a decisive factor in the child's choice to take after the father more than the mother or vice versa. This is a subtle process, both psychological and physiological, that really cannot be approached using the crude methods of the current scientific theory of heredity."[159])

One of the developing attributes of school readiness that culminates at the end of the first seven years is the child's ability to concentrate on the other person *deliberately and attentively*. Imitation, which is still active as an "internal organizing force" during the early years of childhood, acquires a new quality in the first seven-year period's second half. Rudolf Steiner once said that "real imitation" sets in only then. Around the fifth year or so, children begin to direct their energies "deliberately" toward what emanates from the people around them[160]—a process connected to the ongoing metamorphosis of etheric image-forming forces into forces of soul development. Educators and caregivers have already been facing the task and challenge of dealing with the child as a being who perceives, imitates, and relates comprehensively since birth *at the latest*.[161] Now, however, this task takes on a new and different dimension.

4.

Education:
The Challenge and the Approach

In anthroposophical developmental anthropology, imitation and the capacity for it are essential characteristics not only of the first seven-year period, but also those of any *education* in this period of childhood.

> We need to sit down with the children and demonstrate what they are supposed to do—really demonstrate it ourselves—so they need only to imitate it. Prior to the second dentition, all education and teaching must be based on the principle of imitation.[162]

Rudolf Steiner was aware of the fragility of this fundamental process amid the realities of twentieth-century civilization and of how endangered it would be in times to come. The hectic pace of life for parents and their preoccupation with other responsibilities and obligations; the impoverishment of public life in cities and villages, where it is no longer possible to visit artisans and tradespeople at their work, as was still the case in Goethe's time; the electrification and digitization of countless processes formerly performed by human beings—in full view—for others to perceive and experience; the deliberately encouraged abstraction and intellectualization of early childhood life and learning—all of these and numerous other phenomena, tendencies, and intentions, Steiner predicted, would increasingly undermine and override any imitative capacities children would still possess in the future, replacing them with a state of "inactivity and atrophy."

"It is a greater blessing for children...the more they can live, not in their own souls, but in the soul or souls of their surroundings,"[163] said Dr. Steiner and stressed the importance of resisting the "ahrimanic" trend[164] already described (while being fully aware of its universal dominance) by recreating living environments that acknowledge and accommodate the developmental principles of child anthropology. Rudolf Steiner frequently spoke to parents, educators, and other interested individuals about these connections, because he recognized the importance, even the indispensability, of reversing this trend, and about constructively counterbalancing the rapid progress of mechanization, dehumanization, and impoverishment in children's lives and experiences by facilitating and developing experiential spaces that do justice to children and their development, all while avoiding the call to return to irrevocably outdated circumstances. Steiner's concerns went beyond increased "opportunities" for "free time" and "activities," though those are not without value. Rather, he was concerned with restructuring the entire education system in view of the relevance of the considered context. In one of his lecture courses on education, he said,

> In the past, when human life was more instinctual, it was also possible to rely instinctively on this imitation. That will not be the case in the future. Then we will have to take care to ensure that children become imitators, and the never-ending question in education will be how best to structure children's lives so they imitate their surroundings in the best possible way. *As we move into the future, we will have to insist, with increasing forcefulness and awareness,* upon everything that happened in the past with regard to this imitation.[165]

As Rudolf Steiner's explanations of this complex of subjects indicate, we are dealing not only with children's soul development, but also (and most essentially) with their developing *bodily nature*, which lays the foundation for all later development of soul and spirit.

The ultimate goal of the undermining and eroding attack on the child's capacity for imitation, along with its exploitation by advertising and commercialism, is to deform and surreptitiously alienate human bodily nature with the prospect of appropriating it to serve powers other than those of the individual's "I." Rudolf Steiner's pedagogical presentations, unlike his general anthroposophical and esoteric lectures, seldom mentioned the spiritual circumstances behind these events, placing more emphasis on concrete descriptions of what could and had to be done. In his first spiritual-scientifically based discussions of education (in 1906/07, more than twelve years before the founding of the first Waldorf school), he used a simple example, contrasting a purchased, industrially manufactured doll with the product of the child's own imagination:

> We are never again as open to imitation as we are in these first seven years. That is why it is important to influence sense activity during this period, to entice it to emerge, to stimulate it into independent activity. That is also why it is such a mistake to give a young child a nice, "fancy" doll: It does not allow the child's inner forces to become active.

In any case, a child who is developing naturally will reject that doll, preferring a chunk of wood or the like, which stimulates imagination to become inwardly and independently active.[166]

We can make a doll by rolling up an old napkin— two corners become legs, the two others, arms, and a knot with dots of ink for eyes, nose, and mouth becomes the head. Alternatively, we can purchase a "fancy" doll with real hair and tinted cheeks and give that to the child. In engaging with that rolled-up napkin, the child must use her/his imagination to complete the object and make it appear human. This imaginative effort works to shape the brain, which develops through effort just as hand muscles develop through appropriate work. When a child receives a "fancy" doll, the brain has nothing more to do, so it atrophies and withers instead of developing. If people were able to look into the developing brain, as spiritual scientists do, and see its developing forms, they would surely give their children only toys that are designed to stimulate and enliven the brain's sculptural activity. All of this leads to lively inner activity in the organs, which in turn encourages the development of their appropriate forms."[167]

As a realist, Rudolf Steiner was sufficiently aware of the impact and power with which industry and the economy would continue their conquering march through civilization in the absence of any reorientation of social developments. From the beginning, he saw the Waldorf school as part of a larger movement oriented toward *society as a whole*.[168]

On the other hand—especially in view of the existing and ongoing distribution of power—Steiner voted for starting a concrete institution. This institution was the successful establishment of the Waldorf school—all opposing forces notwithstanding—a school designed to be devoted to the development of childhood and not to any other interests or powers. The joy, as well as the profound seriousness, with which he accompanied and promoted the school's growth was noteworthy from the beginning.[169] In a lecture on education after the opening of the Stuttgart Waldorf School, he said,

> It is also possible to kill something off, and whatever is killed in childhood remains dead for all of human life between birth and death. Whatever we allow or encourage to be viable, however, will be there, fresh and blooming, for all of the person's life, and that is the task of a true educator.[170]

Children entered the Waldorf school only at the end of their first seven years, *after* the actual period of imitation and *"formative upbringing."*[171] Nonetheless, the school was also able to provide stimuli for the years prior to school entry, especially by opening a Waldorf kindergarten, which was planned in association with the school from the beginning, and by reaching out to families with younger children through educational lectures, seminars, and other activities designed to instruct parents. Moreover, Steiner repeatedly emphasized that the child's focus on the senses, perception, and imitation does not end abruptly with school entry; in fact, the child's focused attentiveness achieves a high point of sorts in the last phase of the first seven-year period and is therefore preeminently important for the first few school years.

From the very beginning, the Waldorf school's instructional methods, as Steiner conceived them, took the continued availability of imitation into account. Instructional content is generated directly from the artistic element and "real life," not through abstraction. Especially during the first few years of schooling, it continues to build on the available riches of the world children experience through imitation—a world whose different areas of knowledge are then systematically developed through instruction so the children can make them their own under the teacher's guidance. In his educational lectures, Steiner repeatedly emphasized that, during the early school years, lesson contents are internalized in the form of a "wealth of imagery" through the children's fully developed powers of imitation and based on the teacher's authority.

Generally, subjects are presented initially on the basis of images, feelings, and trust in the teacher's personality and are internalized "imitatively," still preserving the relationship-driven learning typical of the preschool years. Spiritual and intellectual reflection on these same subjects comes only later, after the midpoint of childhood in early adolescence. In a lecture series on education, Steiner had this to say about the guidelines and leading thoughts of Waldorf education:

> If at all possible, education must ensure that the intellectual element that awakens at puberty can find nourishment within the person's own being. If children first acquire an inner wealth of images through imitation and on the basis of authority, that wealth can then be transformed intellectually once they reach puberty—the point when they are faced with beginning ability to *think* what they formerly *willed* and *felt*. A fundamental concern of instruction and child rearing is to ensure that this intellectual thinking does not set in too early. Individuals do not come to an experience of freedom through any attempt on our part to force-feed

them, but only through what awakens spontaneously within them. That should not, however, awaken to soul poverty. If people have absorbed nothing through imitation earlier in life, nothing that can emerge into thinking from the soul's depths, and then attempt to continue to develop their thinking during adolescence, they then find nothing to support that development. Their thinking is left grasping at straws, so to speak, and is unstable because it lacks a foundation.[172]

At no point did Rudolf Steiner aspire to a pedagogical method for the twentieth century and beyond that would not adequately accommodate the awakening capacity of children and adolescents to think and judge. The just-cited statements (and some comparable passages in lectures) are definitely not to be construed as rejecting children's thinking prior to puberty. Steiner himself, as a spiritually precocious child, lived and struggled with the emergence of profound questions during the first seven years of his life, but he found no one capable of sharing or understanding them—a fact that caused him many years of suffering.[173] For him, however, the important point in his discussions on education was to create a concrete alternative to the dominant style of teaching and child-rearing, which one-sidedly emphasized, addressed, and fostered cognitive–intellectual principles and the capacity for consciousness in the individual's biography at the expense of self-forgetful play or other creative activities.

Overall, the goal of Waldorf education was (and remains) to promote an individual style of thinking and judging that is not bound solely by abstract intellectual perspectives, but is "existential" in character—connected to (and responsible to) the impulses and values of feeling and willing. Instruction at the end of the first seven-year period (and well beyond, into the middle of childhood, a developmental period of pronounced psychological internalization[174]) has to do with fostering the development of feeling and willing in this way, achieving exceptional results through forms of play and art that are appropriate (on the level of developmental physiology) to the continued activity of the sensory–imitative principle and contribute significantly to the "wealth" that adolescents will be able to draw on later for independent thinking and introspection.

Another aspect of the maturing child's potential wealth is a "feeling," force, or "virtue" that arises in the context of successful imitation in adequate surroundings and can permeate all the rest of children's existence and their relationship to the world, whether on the level of body, soul, or spirit. Rudolf Steiner called the *feeling of gratitude* a "primal virtue" and a pillar of human life and said that it is neither "inherited" nor brought into earthly life from the pre-birth state, nor is it acquired through admonishment or moral training. Rather, it comes about in the process of imitative internalization, through an active and receptive connection to the world. During the time when children are not yet self-aware, their individual bodily nature develops through (and on the basis of) experiences prepared for them and made possible by their attachment figures. This is how children receive essential aspects of the surroundings in which they live, develop, and participate.

Later, having passed through several stages of increasing consciousness, this entire process can lead to a sense of gratitude for what has been received, for the aspects of individual personality it has fostered—in short, for the "dialogue" process. Long before this feeling of gratitude emerges into consciousness, however, it can already illuminate the child's existence, as Rudolf Steiner emphasized to educators in Dornach on April 20, 1923:

> If the virtue of gratitude is to express itself fully in the human soul, it must grow with the person, flow into the person at the stage when the inward-directed growth forces are most vital and flexible. Gratitude is something that must develop from

the bodily–religious aspect I described as prevailing in children from birth to the second dentition. In fact, it can develop all by itself during this period of life if the child is raised appropriately. If what flows into the child through imitation then flows outward into the surroundings in appropriate devotion and love to the child's parents or other caregivers, it is also truly imbued with gratitude. If I may put it like this, when we ourselves simply behave in ways that are worthy of thanks, that gratitude will also stream toward us from the children, especially in the first period of life. Later, as this gratitude develops and matures, it flows into the growth forces that make the limbs lengthen and even alter the chemical composition of the blood and other body fluids.

Gratitude lives in the body, as indeed it must, since otherwise it is not adequately grounded in the person. It would be wrong to urge children to be thankful for what their surroundings bestow on them. Rather, we must help gratitude to flow naturally by allowing children to see how even we adults experience and express gratitude when other people give freely of themselves. In other words, a feeling of gratitude should prevail in the children's surroundings, and we should help them become accustomed to imitating it. Saying "Thank you" spontaneously and often—not because they are told to, but through imitation—will have exceptionally positive effects on children's over-all development. We often pay too little attention to the feeling of gratitude that consolidates dur-ing the first period of childhood, but once pres-ent it develops into a comprehensive, universal sense of gratitude toward the whole world. It is extremely important for people to acquire grati-tude toward the world. It need not always rise to the level of consciousness but can remain on the level of unconscious feeling as, for example, when we encounter a beautiful flower-strewn meadow after a strenuous hike. On the level of uncon-scious feeling, a sense of gratitude can appear for everything we see in nature, such as the Sun rising anew every morning.

If we behave as we should in the presence of children, they gradually develop gratitude for everything other people give them and say to them, for how people smile at them and treat them, and so forth. This universal sense of gratitude is the foundation of a truly religious attitude.[175]

According to Rudolf Steiner, a second soul–spiri-tual essential of human life on both the interpersonal and the cosmic levels is *respect*—respect for the other person or for the Other as a fellow human being. The groundwork for respect is also laid through years of successful perception and imitation in early childhood, and it, too, can later become a "cardinal virtue." In developmental physiology and psychology, as Rudolf Steiner indicated, early childhood experiences of imitation pave the way for "the right respect, for showing the right appreciation for the other person, for making the effort to give other people the regard and appreciation they deserve simply because each of them has a human face."[176] Children adapt to interpersonal life through their ready capacity for imitation, through successful interaction with and adaptation to the Other in their intimate circle—a person whose "gestures" they internalize. This "other," although perhaps initially the child's sole or central attachment figure, is the representative of a larger whole and, as such, certainly provides the impetus for many inner developments that later come to bear on other social connections. As development proceeds apace, children encounter many more (and many different) "others;" ultimately, through interacting with these "others," they experience what it means to be a human individual.

In this *gratitude* for what the world provides and in this *respect* for the human individual who conveys and opens up this world to the child (in the sense not of mere knowledge but of authentic participation in existence, which extends to the development of the child's own physical nature). Seen against this anthropological backdrop, gratitude and respect can be understood as attitudes or capacities that have persisted in interpersonal life for centuries or even millennia, regardless of differences in religious, philosophical, or political systems, because their foundations are laid in the experiences of early childhood. From this perspective, the often dramatic decline of gratitude and respect in modern civilization actually has little to do with postmodern atheism and the destruction of the "image of the human being" in this age of scientific reductionism, which views "gratitude" toward Creation as an archaic relic of ancient theistic values, while "respect" implies underestimation of biologically determined drives.

According to Steiner's thoughts on developmental anthropology, the decline of these essentials, or "cardinal virtues," has much more to do with the fact that children are being deprived of essential modes of experience in early childhood, which in turn is related to interference in their surroundings, as described earlier in this chapter. When imitation is systematically prevented and discouraged, undermined and reduced, a different, dehumanized, and potentially dangerous world emerges.

≈

This chapter began with a quotation from Rudolf Steiner:

> The never-ending question in education will be how best to structure children's lives so they imitate their surroundings in the best possible way. As we move into the future, we will have to insist, with increasing forcefulness and awareness, upon everything that happened in the past with regard to this imitation.

Rudolf Steiner described the need for "formative education" during the first seven years of life, emphasizing the importance of appropriate spheres of life and experience that need to be developed anew in the midst of a world of changing technology and soul impoverishment. He repeatedly makes it clear what kind of self-education is demanded of educators now and in future. His impressive descriptions of children's imitative participation in the "gestures" of their caregivers made his listeners and readers (who included the members of the Teachers' College of the first Waldorf school) conscious of how much depended on them and on their inner world of soul and spirit, since children actually participate in this world and are at least partially dependent on it for their bodily development.

> From what we do in their presence, children sense the thoughts underlying a gesture or hand

movement. They sense this not by "interpreting" gestures, of course, but through a much more active inner connection to the adult than any that exists later between adults. As a result, we cannot allow ourselves to feel or think anything in a child's presence that should not continue to resonate in the child. During the child's early years, our behavior as educators must be governed absolutely by this principle: In the child's presence, everything you yourself experience—right down into your sensing, feeling, and thinking—must be such that it can continue to resonate in the child. In childhood, therefore, the psychologist, the soul-observer, the experienced adult, and the physician are one, because everything that makes an impression and provokes a soul reaction in children extends into their circulation, digestion, and so on, forming the foundation for constitutional health later in life. When we educate on the level of soul and spirit, counting on the child's capacity for imitation, we also educate the living body. A wonderful metamorphosis occurs here: What approaches the child on the spirit and soul levels is transformed into the child's physical, organic constitution and predisposition to health or illness later in life.[177]

Thus, Rudolf Steiner pointed out what the educator's attitude must be, now and in the future: "*In the*

child's presence, everything you yourself experience—
right down into your sensing, feeling, and thinking—
must be such that it can continue to resonate in the
child."

In a different setting, Steiner said that the "feeling
for this state of affairs" and the "attitude" this feeling engenders are what actually make an educator,[178]
although at present this principle is rarely recognized or
acknowledged, let alone put into practice, even among
educators. "This principle of doing nothing, saying
nothing, and even thinking nothing that might cause
harm to the child who imitates it is still really not at all
prevalent."[179] In many lectures, especially those given
to teachers and parents, Rudolf Steiner described the
real effects of an educator's unschooled soul life on the
child's physical development—less with regard to one-
time derailments than to habitual patterns (primarily in
the realm of temperament) that are acted out as such.
Taking the example of an educator or attachment figure
with a naturally choleric temperament, he said:

> Suppose something really blatant happens in the
> child's presence—an outburst of anger; someone
> gets furious. The whole child then has an inner
> picture of this outburst; the ether body con-
> structs an image related to the outburst, which

then passes into all of the child's circulatory system and vascular metabolism. That is how it works during the first seven years, and the child's organism adapts accordingly.[180]

Steiner sketched the development of a variety of major health problems as the delayed effects of early-childhood experiences of attachment figures with uncontrolled tempers, emphasizing that the manifestations appear in the second half of life. He called repeatedly for extensive scientific studies to research and document these connections so important for public health. ("There will come a time when doctoral theses will deal with cases such as this: An incident of illness at age forty-eight, with symptoms X and Y, is traced back to ugly thoughts of a particular sort that the child encountered in the fourth or fifth year. Insights such as this will allow us to approach the human being truly and thus gain an overview of all of human life."[181])

Steiner held the view that, in the future, existing connections (the "wonderful metamorphosis of what approaches the child on the spirit and soul levels to be transformed into the person's physical, organic constitution and predisposition to health or illness in later life") will be increasingly acknowledged and taken into account, allowing the emergence of a new consciousness of—and, as appropriate, a society-wide reflection on—the significance of imitative processes in childhood and educational conditions during the first seven-year period.

Rudolf Steiner's interest did not lie primarily in being proven right (or in having his statements "evaluated" and "confirmed") but rather in altering the course of the present and the future—in this case, the circumstances of children's life and schooling during early childhood and the first years of school—as long as that remained possible. Thus his suggestions about future medical and epidemiological studies were more or less asides, aphoristic comments embedded in educational lectures that focused on a change of consciousness among educators, parents, and teachers *here and now*—a shift in consciousness based on insight. If they succeeded among themselves in awaking an understanding of the nature and significance of imitative processes in childhood—that is, of the child "as sense organ"—in the context of a new anthropology of childhood, many of them would draw the consequences themselves in their educational attitude and self-schooling, as well as in their work with the children. And to Steiner, *that* was the most important and urgent point.

Appendix: Imitation and Life before Birth

Prior to the second dentition, we can still clearly perceive the aftereffects of the child's lifestyle and habits in the spiritual world before birth or even conception. The child's body behaves almost as if it were spirit, because the spirit that has descended from the spiritual world is still fully active in the child during the first seven years of life.[182]

In an educational lecture in Stuttgart, April 9, 1924, Rudolf Steiner spoke about the state of the child's incarnation during the first seven years of life:

> Then this being with its spiritual experiences descends, uniting—loosely at first—with the physical human element during the embryonic period. In the first period of life, between birth and the second dentition, it remains loosely and superficially attached, like an aura hovering around the person. This being of spirit and soul that descends from the spiritual world is just as real as what we

see emerging from the mother's body, but because it is still more loosely associated with the child's physical nature than it will be later, the child still lives "outside the body" to a greater extent than is the case with the adult.[183]

During the first seven years, the actual being of the child is still located largely "outside the body," "hovering" around it like an "aura," "loosely connected" to an enlivened physical body into which it incarnates step by step. This process proceeds from the head downward and is marked by several milestones: *sensory maturity* (in the first seven years), *respiratory maturity* (in the second seven years), and the *earthly maturity* of adolescence.[184] As Rudolf Steiner describes elsewhere, the spirit and soul element's "loose connection" to the living body prior to the second dentition is also the constitutional basis of early childhood's signature "all sense organ" status.[185]

Impressions from the environment trickle throughout the entire organism, resonating and reverberating, because the child's looser spirit and soul element lives in the surroundings; its connection to the body is not yet as intimate as is the case in adults. That is why all impressions from the surroundings are so readily received.[186]

According to anthroposophical anthropology, the child's individuality reincarnates out of a post-death, pre-birth world into earthly existence. Coming from a purely spiritual sphere of existence and experience, this being takes many years of development to find its way into the forces and functions of earthly existence. It must "in-*carnate*"—enter the flesh—to participate in the unfolding of earthly forces and characteristics with the help of the body. As emphasized earlier, this process is a two-way street: Through active participation, the "I" incarnates further into the body, as Rudolf Steiner demonstrated in his studies of human uprightness, walking, speaking, and thinking. The continued activity of prenatal cosmic forces and life processes also still plays an important role in this process.[187]

All of the "bodily–religious devotion to the environment,"[188] the "religious soul-orientation still so entirely grounded in the body,"[189] that is so typical of children is related to the active character of the individuality's experiences in the prenatal world. The "basic trust" that was such an intense topic of concern for psychoanalysis beginning in the late nineteenth century—that is, the child's receptive nature ("all sense organ") and almost absolute attachment to the primary caregiver—does not arise from any *earthly* experiences (for which it rather constitutes the prerequisites) but from events and life-processes in the spiritual world prior to conception. In one description of the human individuality and its path from death to rebirth, Rudolf Steiner said:

> Imaginative activity is especially well developed in the first period after passage through the gates of death, when a comprehensive world of images unrolls before us in the form of Imaginations. In contrast, the second third of life between death and rebirth is filled primarily with Inspirations. Inspirations appear during the second half of human life between death and rebirth, and Intuitions in the final third.
>
> Now, Intuitions consist of instilling the human self, the soul aspect, into other beings, and this process culminates in infiltrating a physical body. Merging into a physical body through birth is simply an extension of the largely intuitive activity of the last third of life between death and rebirth. Thus, when a human being enters physical existence, the ability to merge the Self into the Other necessarily appears as an especially characteristic trait of early childhood. Little children *must* do what others do; rather than acting out of themselves, they imitate the actions of others.

In my lecture "The Education of the Child in the Light of Spiritual Science," why did I describe children under the age of seven as imitators first and foremost? Because imitation, the ability to insert oneself into others, is simply the continuation of the intuitive world of the final third of life between death and rebirth. Thoughtful observation of the life of young children reveals that life between death and rebirth is still streaming into them, radiating into them. (Munich, May 4, 1918)[190]

Rudolf Steiner took up this perspective again in the fall of 1919 when the Waldorf school was being established. In one of his educational lectures, he said that after being born into physical existence, children simply carry on with what they experienced prior to conception in spiritual worlds, where they lived in intimate "intuitive" connection with the beings of the higher hierarchies. They actually lived *in* those beings and obeyed their impulses: "Under these circumstances, we are imitators to a much greater degree because we are one with the beings we are imitating." After birth, upon entering physical existence, the child's individuality retains its intuitive existential constitution—or "habit" of "being one with the environment"—to a certain extent: "This habit extends to being one with or imitating the beings present in the surroundings, namely, people who serve as caregivers, whose actions, thoughts, and feelings should then all be worthy of imitation by the child."[191]

In a different context, in a general anthroposophical lecture in October 1920, Rudolf Steiner then said that imitation is therefore essentially nothing more than "the *continued activity* of something present in a very different form in the spiritual world prior to birth or conception, namely, the immersion of one being in another. It is then expressed in children's imitation of their human surroundings as a *lingering reverberation of spiritual experience.*"[192]

Before entering earthly existence, the human individuality's spiritual experience was full of "devotion," or "self-surrender." This attitude continues or reverberates as children enter the earthly world and submit to their environment through imitation.[193] Thus "basic trust," according to Steiner's first lecture course for the Stuttgart Waldorf teachers, consists of the fact that children actually do trust in the "morality of the world" and therefore are also confident that it is worthy of imitation.[194] In a later presentation, Steiner also said, "In all instances, children entering the world as imitative creatures pronounce the judgment, 'I believe in the goodness of the world that has received me.' This is an unconscious judgment on the part of every child."[195] Children, Steiner tells us, set out on the path through earthly life against the backdrop of their prenatal experiences and intuitive activity and with a concrete, substantial *sense of truth*, which must then be addressed and further developed in the right way in school:

> Consider this: In the first few years of life, children are still embedded in the spiritual world and apply its principles in attempting to become comfortable in the outer world. This is when children acquire the sense of truth. As they make their way into the world, their basic assessment of it is this: The things around me are just as true as everything that appeared to me, transparent and illumined, in the spiritual world. The sense of truth develops even before children enter school. In school, we experience the final phases of that development and must then give this sense of truth an appropriate reception. If we fail to do so, we stunt children's sense of truth instead of encouraging its further development.[196]

Despite all the quotations cited here and all the summations of Rudolf Steiner's comments on the "sense organ" quality of children and their astonishing capacity for imitation, Steiner seldom spoke in explicit detail about the prenatal spiritual background. On the occasions in question, he was clearly not concerned with giving his audience of teachers and parents a full overview of anthroposophical anthropology with all of its cosmic

implications. Rather, his orientation was primarily phenomenological, providing only what was immediately
necessary and relevant for their educational work. It
was obvious, however, that Steiner hoped that a more
intensive study and development of the overarching
context would be pursued, at least by the teachers of
the Independent Waldorf School, since there could be
no doubt about its importance for their work and their
inner attitude:

> *Teachers, however, should know about this. They*
> *should face the child with tremendous reverence*
> *and know that they are encountering a divine*
> *spiritual being descended to Earth. Everything*
> *depends on us knowing this, filling our hearts*
> *with it, and becoming educators on that basis.*[197]

Notes

NOTE: "CW" refers to volume number in The Collected Works of Rudolf Steiner (see "Works Cited" (pages 96–103).

1   Cf. SPITZ 1996.
2   Cf. RITTELMEYER 2005, p. 49 and the image, reproduced there, from a hospital film by Spitz.
3   As quoted in RITTELMEYER, ibid., p. 50.
4   Cf. BRETHERTON, INGE: Die Geschichte der Bindingstheorie. In: SPANGLER 1997, p. 27ff.
5   Cf. GROSSMANN 2003.
6   RITTELMEYER 2005, p. 70.
7   FUCHS 2008a, p. 23.
8   Ibid., p. 49.
9   Cf. PIAGET 1978.
10   FUCHS op. cit., p. 18.
11   Cf. FUCHS 2000, pp. 111 and 126, for his use of the term "incarnation."
12   FUCHS 2008a, p. 30.
13   Cf. ibid., pp. 248ff. and 275ff.
14   For summaries, see BAUER 2005 and FUCHS 2008B, pp. 195ff.
15   FUCHS 2000, p. 249.
16   FUCHS 2008a, p. 59. For more detail, see FUCHS 2008b.
17   Cf. RITTELMEYER 2005, p. 78.
18   CW 330, p. 306
19   CW 84, pp. 199ff.
20   CW 298, p. 209.
21   CW 301, p. 45.

22   CW 192, p. 285. For details, cf. also SELG 2012, pp.
      1477ff.
23   CW 293, pp. 27ff.
24   Cf. SELG 2011a, 2011b, 2011c, 2012, 2013, 2015.
25   Cf. CW 21; cf. also SELG 2012a, pp. 1166–1206 for a
      discussion of this work by Rudolf Steiner.
26   CW 149, p. 112.
27   CW 304a, p. 96.
28   CW 311, p. 15.
29   Ibid.
30   Ibid., p. 17.
31   Ibid., p. 16. Steiner then continues in more detail: "There
      you are [in the spiritual world in its spiritual substance]
      as if in a spiritual garment all your own, and now you are
      supposed to descend to earth, to select a body on earth.
      This body has been in preparation for generations: A
      father and a mother had a son or a daughter who in turn
      had a son or a daughter, and so on. The result is a body
      developed through heredity, and now you are supposed
      to move into it. All of a sudden, you enter into completely
      different circumstances as you put on this body that has
      been prepared for you through generations. Of course, you
      have been working down from the spiritual world to ensure
      that you do not receive a completely unsuitable body. Still,
      the body you get is usually not a very good match for you;
      you don't fit into it well. If a glove fit you as poorly as
      bodies typically do, you would simply toss that glove away.
      It wouldn't even occur to you to put it on. But when you
      are descending from the spiritual world and want to have a
      body, you must take what you get." (ibid., p. 17)
32   Ibid., p. 19.
33   CW 293, p. 24.
34   Ibid., p. 25. For details, cf. KRANICH 1999, pp. 160–179,
      and LEBER 2002, pp. 63–120.

35   GA 293, p. 26.

36   Ibid.

37   CW 302a, p. 63.

38   Ibid.

39   Ibid., pp. 63ff.

40   CW 311, p. 116.

41   CW 316, p. 201.

42   CW 218, p. 245.

43   CW 276, p. 142.

44   CW 218, p. 55.

45   GA 303, pp. 157ff.

46   CW 314, p. 135. For the history of this volume, cf. SELG 2006, pp. 714ff. ["The polarity of head and metabolic forces and their significance in shaping the organs"]

47   For Rudolf Steiner's characterization of the members of the human constitution in the context of human physiology, cf. SELG 2006, pp. 97ff. and 460ff.

48   CW 302a, p. 26.

49   CW 304a, p. 99.

50   CW 308, p. 48.

51   CW 304a, p. 35.

52   CW 210, p. 233.

53   CW 317, p. 101.

54   CW 315, p. 99.

55   CW 317, p. 14.

56   CW 314, p. 147.

57   CW 305, p. 62.

58   CW 304, pp. 35ff.

59   CW 312, p. 241.

60   CW 306, p. 63.

61   CW 304, pp. 142ff.

62   Ibid., pp. 166ff.

63   Ibid.,p. 144.

64   CW 26, p. 256.

65 CW 311, pp. 15ff.

66 CW 302a, p. 52.

67 CW 304, pp. 147ff.

68 CW 306, p. 45.

69 Cf. CW 311, pp. 16ff.

70 CW 310, p. 45.

71 On the head system's relationship to the past, cf. SELG 2006, pp. 362ff.

72 CW 201, p. 115.

73 CW 297, p. 165.

74 For more on the polarity of blood and nerve, sympathy and antipathy, cf. CW 293, pp. 34ff.; LEBER 2002, pp. 206ff.; and SELG 2006, pp. 636ff.

75 CW 307, p. 47. On the relationship of the milk teeth to the head system and of the secondary teeth to ascending forces out of the body, cf. CW 201, pp. 114ff.

76 CW 311, p. 96.

77 CW 308, pp. 28ff.

78 CW 311, p. 19. For more on Rudolf Steiner's discussion of the "body template" and its transformation, cf. SELG 2004, pp.147ff., and SELG 2006, pp. 719ff.

79 CW 308, p. 23.

80 On the transformation of the physical body during the first seven years and on the development of new teeth from the perspective of scientific and anthropological findings, c.f. KRANICH 1992, pp. 81ff. (Reprinted in KRANICH 1999, pp. 95ff.

81 CW 304a, p. 94.

82 CW 302a, pp. 26ff.

83 CW 305, p. 235.

84 Ibid., p. 157.

85 "If we consider the gradual release of certain of the ether body's forces in approximately the first seven years of life, we can see how the ether body becomes free to serve the

head around two-and-a-half years after birth, the chest around the fifth year, and the metabolic–limb system from then until the secondary dentition." (CW 303, pp. 126ff.)

86 CW 302a, p. 54.
87 CW 81, p. 81.
88 CW 34, p. 328.
89 CW 84, p. 198.
90 CW 304, p. 198.
91 CW 315, p. 114.
92 CW 306, p. 43.
93 CW 304a, p. 97.
94 Cf. CW 293, p. 83.
95 CW 304a, p. 35.
96 CW 305, p. 54.
97 CW 308, p.14.
98 CW 303, p. 276.
99 CW 218, p. 247.
100 CW 308, p. 14.
101 CW 212, p. 111.
102 CW 218, p. 229. Cf. note 186.
103 CW 304a, p. 34.
104 Cf. MÜLLER-WIEDEMANN 1989 and SELG 2011a.
105 CW 304, pp. 149ff.
106 Cf. also KRANICH 1999, pp.56ff.
107 CW 306, p. 72.
108 CW CW297a, p. 154.
109 CW 306, p. 52.
110 CW 308, p.30.
111 CW 297a, p. 153.
112 Ibid.
113 Cf. also KRANICH 1992, p. 70: "Perception, soul-submission, and will activity form a unity that breaks apart only later, once decision-based action begins. Within this unity, children are so receptive to their environment that

it works into areas of the body where will is involuntarily activated."

114   CW 218, p. 247.

115   CW 308, p. 15.

116   CW 305, p. 58.

117   CW 218, p.55.

118   Ibid., pp. 63ff.

119   CW 293, pp. 111ff.

120   CW 309a, p. 108.

121   CW 306, p. 96.

122   Cf. CW 305, pp. 15ff; CW 293, p. 83; and LEBER 2002, pp. 614ff.

123   CW 304a, p. 108.

124   Ibid.

125   CW 306, p. 51.

126   CW 304a, p. 108.

127   CW 84, p. 199. On seeing and hearing as examples of the intertwining of perception, movement, and imitation and the (unconscious) will dimension of the entire process, cf. KRANICH 1992, p. 70: "The eye takes in the colors coming from an object by allowing them to penetrate the whole organ. For a perception of the object to develop, however, the eye must track the object with movements so subtle we normally do not notice them. The mental images contained in any perception of an object develop hrough these movements. We can see the object only because we recreate its form through eye movements. Similarly, we can hear a melody only by inwardly accompanying the steps of the intervals. Thus perception always involves a subtle will activity in the sense organs that 'imitates' the forms and movements we perceive." Karl König was the first to discuss the interaction of perception and movement (as well as the sense of self-movement) from the anthroposophical perspective in connection both with Rudolf Steiner's

Notes

teachings on the senses and with recent studies in sense
physiology, including those coming out of Viktor von
Weizsäcker's Heidelberg School, all of which König
incorporated into his own teachings on child development.
(Cf. König 1971, pp. 55ff.) For Steiner's perspectives, see
in particular CW 21, pp. 143ff., and CW 293, pp. 134ff.
("When we see a colored circle, we may put it roughly
like this: I see the color, and I also see the circle's curve,
its circular shape. When we do so, however, two totally
different things are being jumbled up together. Through the
eye's own inherent and isolated activity, you initially see
only the color. You see the circular shape by subconsciously
applying your sense of movement, unconsciously tracing
a circular motion in the ether body and astral body and
then raising it into consciousness. The shape you have
recognized as a circle unites with the color you perceived
only once the circle you have taken in through your sense
of movement rises into consciousness. In other words, you
retrieve the shape from your entire body by appealing to
the sense of movement , which is spread out throughout the
body.") Cf. also SELG 2006, pp. 552 ff, "The interaction of
the individual senses."

128   CW 297, p. 163.
129   CW 304, p. 195.
130   CW 305, p. 15.
131   CW 306, p. 96.
132   CW 24, p. 86.
133   CW 55, p. 164.
134   CW 297a, pp. 196ff.
135   CW 304a, p. 34.
136   TAULER 1987, p. 20.
137   FUCHS 2000, p. 316.
138   CW 309, pp. 41ff. For more about the changes in ideation
      and memory in the child at this age, cf. KRANICH (1992,

pp. 83ff.), among others: "Even when five-year-olds look at things, the mental images that form still dissolve very rapidly. In preschoolers, memory is still very labile. In contrast, seven-year-olds are able to hold on to mental images and to summon them up again at will—i.e., to redevelop them in the process of remembering—even *after* seeing objects. This memory is an internal image-shaping process that takes place when a child who is capable of later recalling images looks at things. Mental images are transformed into structured images when their transient shapes are imbued with form-giving energy. In addition to direct perception and experience of the outer world, the child now develops an inner world of images that not only permit experiences to be recalled at will in memory but also give form (in imagination) to things not seen." On Rudolf Steiner's description of the activity of mental-image memory, in sharp distinction to "memory that becomes organic (= internalization) in the child prior to the second dentition" (CW 323, p. 66), cf. also LEBER 1993, pp. 278 ff. ("Habit and memory"); on the history of this work, cf. SELG 2006, pp. 654ff. ("The significance of physical–etheric bodily processes for the development of human memory and recall")

139   FUCHS 2008a, p. 43.

140   CW 217, p. 160.

141   CW 293, p. 161.

142   In this connection, S. Leber quotes Hans Carossa, whose autobiographical memoirs (*A Childhood,* 1932) recount a three-year-old's experience of the eagerly anticipated appearance of a comet: "People waiting patiently, staring, whispering almost anxiously; the lonely lingering of that curving gleam in the distance—all this made a lasting impression but took hold of me much more strongly later, in recollection, than it did on that night. At barely three

years old, I was not developed enough for either fear or delight; *my mother held me up, perched on her arm, and I sensed the secure, reliable course of the world through her."* (LEBER 1993, p. 220; italics added)

143 CW 310, p. 49.
144 CW 306, p. 58.
145 CW 310, p. 49.
146 CW 306, p. 126.
147 CW 308, p. 14.
148 CW 115, p. 86.
149 CW 298, p. 208.
150 Cf. the over view of Steiner's key perspectives in SELG 2006, pp. 708–714, and in KÖNIG's foundational study (1957).
151 CW 310, p. 46ff.
152 CW 303, p. 127.
153 CW 297, p. 163.
154 Ibid., p. 256.
155 CW 304a, p.34ff.
156 As quoted in SELG 2015, p. 115.
157 Ibid., p. 69.
158 Ibid.
159 CW 306, p. 51.
160 CW 297, p. 255.
161 For information on the results of early twenty-first century research on *prenatal* development with regard to human connections, cf. the succinct summary of findings in prenatal psychology and embryology in RITTELMEYER 2005, pp. 9–43.
162 CW 310, p. 52.
163 CW 296, p. 18.
164 For Rudolf Steiner's anthroposophical perspectives on the multilayered dimension of evil and the adversarial activity of the forces of the Antichrist, cf. in particular

PROKOFIEFF 2013, pp. 287ff. For medical and developmental physiological perspectives, cf. SELG 2001, pp. 59ff.

165   CW 296, p. 18.

166   CW 95, p. 55.

167   CW 34, p.325.

168   Cf. e.g. SCHMELZER 1991 and SELG 2012a, pp. 1320ff.

169   Cf. SELG 2012, pp. 132ff.

170   CW 304, p. 48.

171   CW 304a, p. 170

172   CW 309, pp. 79ff.

173   Cf. SELG 2012, pp. 60ff.

174   Cf. MÜLLER-WIEDEMANN 1989 and SELG 2011a.

175   CW 306, pp. 116ff.

176   CW 330, p. 279.

177   CW 308, pp. 34ff.

178   CW 304a, p. 35.

179   CW 330, p. 307.

180   CW 311, p. 25

181   CW 309, p. 37. Cf. Steiner's many similar descriptions in SELG 2014, pp. 136–141.

182   CW 311, p. 15.

183   CW 308, p. 17.

184   CW 317, p. 18.

185   Within the human sensory system, the organizational and functional activity of the human constitution's higher members tends to be minimal, favoring their immanence (distant from the body) in the outer world, which is only reflected in and raised to consciousness through physical organs. On the general configuration of this system, cf. SELG 2006, pp. 279ff. and 532ff.

186   CW 308, p. 28.

187 Cf. SELG 1006, pp. 713ff. ("The activity of the members of the human constitution in achieving walking, speaking, and thinking")

188 GA 306, p. 56.

189 Ibid., p. 53.

190 CW 174a, p. 283.

191 CW 296, p. 18.

192 CW 200, p. 115.

193 CW 293, p. 142.

194 Ibid., p. 143. On the spiritual background of the founding of the Stuttgart school in view of the (difficult) prenatal experiences of children born since around 1912, cf. also CW 190, pp. 57ff.; CW 193, pp. 86ff.; and CW 296, pp. 89ff., as well as the summary in SELG 2012a, pp. 1471ff.

195 CW 301, pp. 227ff.

196 CW 302, p. 128.

197 CW 311, pp. 19ff.

Works Cited

BY RUDOLF STEINER

CW 21 *Vom Seelenrätseln,* Dornach 1983. In English: *Riddles of the Soul* (Chestnut Ridge, NY: Mercury Press, 1996).

CW 24 *Aufsätze über die Dreigliederung des sozialen Organismus und zur Zeitlage 1915–1921.* Dornach 1982.

CW 26 *Anthroposophische Leitsätze. Der Erkenntnisweg der Anthroposophie – Das Michael-Mysterium (1924–1925).* Dornach 1998. In English: *Anthroposophical Leading Thoughts* (London: Rudolf Steiner Press, 2007).

CW 34 *Lucifer–Gnosis. Grundlegende Aufsätze zur Anthroposophie und Berichte aus den Zeitschriften «Luzifer» und «Lucifer–Gnosis» 1903–1908.* Dornach 1987.

CW 55 *Die Erkenntnis des Übersinnlichen in unserer Zeit und deren Bedeutung für das heutige Leben (1906/07).* Dornach 1983. In English: *Supersensible Knowledge* (Hudson, NY: Anthroposophic Press, 1987).

CW 81 *Erneuerungs-Impulse für Kultur und Wissenschaft. Berliner Hochschulkurs (1922).* Dornach 1994. In English: *Reimagining Academic Studies* (Great Barrington, MA: SteinerBooks, 2015).

CW 84 *Was wollte das Goetheanum und was soll die Anthroposophie? (1923–1924).* Dornach 1986.

CW 95 *Vor dem Tore der Theosophie (1906).* Dornach 1990.

CW 115 *Anthroposophie – Psychosophie – Pneumatosophie (1909).* Dornach 2001. In English: *A Psychology of Body, Soul, and Spirit* (Hudson, NY: Anthroposophic Press, 1999.

CW 149 *Christus und die geistigen Welt. Von der Suche nach dem heiligen Gral.* In English: *Christ and the Spiritual World: And the Search for the Holy Grail* (London: Rudolf Steiner Press, 2008).

CW 159 *Das Geheimnis des Todes. Wesen und Bedeutung Mitteleuropas und die europäischen Volksgeister (1915).* Dornach 2005.

CW 174a *Mitteleuropa zwischen Ost und West (1914–1918).* Dornach 1982.

CW 190 *Vergangenheits- und Zukunftsimpulse im sozialen Geschehen. Die geistigen Hintergründe der sozialen Frage. Band II (1919).* Dornach 1980.

CW 192 *Geisteswissenschaftliche Behandlung sozialer und pädagogischer Fragen (1919).* Dornach 1991. In English: *Education as a Force for Social Change* (Hudson, NY: Anthroposophic Press, 1997).

CW 193 *Der innere Aspekt des sozialen Rätsels. Luziferische Vergangenheit und ahrimanische Zukunft (1919).* Dornach 2007. In English: *The Esoteric Aspect of the Social Question* (London: Rudolf Steiner Press, 2001).

CW 197 *Gegensätze in der Menschheitsentwicklung. West und Ost–Materialismus und Mystik–Wissen und Glauben (1920).* Dornach 1996.

CW 200 *Die neue Geistigkeit und das Christus-Erlebnis des zwanzigsten Jahrhunderts (1920).* Dornach 2003.

CW 201 *Entsprechungen zwischen Mikrokosmos und Makrokosmos. Der Mensch–eine Hieroglyphe des Weltenalls (1920).* Dornach 1987. In English: *Mystery of the Universe: The Human Being, Model of Creation* (London: Rudolf Steiner Press, 2001).

CW 210 *Alte und neue Einweihungsmethoden. Drama und Dichtung im Bewusstseins-Umschwung der Neuzeit (1922).* Dornach 2001. In English: *Old and New Methods of Initiation* (London: Rudolf Steiner Press, 1967).

CW 212 *Menschliches Seelenleben und Geistesstreben im Zusammenhange mit Welt- und Erdenentwicklung (1922).* Dornach 1998. In Englsih: *Life of the Human Soul* (London: Rudolf Steiner Press, 2017).

CW 217 *Geistige Wirkenskräfte im Zusammenleben von alter und junger Generation. Pädagogischer Jugendkurs (1922).* Dornach 1988. In English: *Becoming the*

Archangel Michael's Companions (Great Barrington, MA: SteinerBooks, 2006).

CW 218 *Geistige Zusammenhänge in der Gestaltung des menschlichen Organismus (1922)*. Dornach 1992. In English: *Spirit as Sculptor of the Human Organism* (London: Rudolf Steiner Press, 2015).

CW 276 *Das Künstlerische in seiner Weltmission. Der Genius der Sprache. Die Welt des sich offenbarenden strahlenden Scheins–Anthroposophie und Kunst. Anthroposophie und Dichtung (1923)*. Dornach 2002. In English: *The Arts and Their Mission* (Hudson, NY: Anthroposophic Press, 1986).

CW 293 *Allgemeine Menschenkunde als Grundlage der Pädagogik (I) (1919)*. Dornach 1992. In English: *The Foundations of Human Experience* (Hudson, NY: Anthroposophic Press, 1996).

CW 296 *Die Erziehungsfrage als soziale Frage (1919)*. Dornach 1991. In English: *Education as a Force for Social Change* (Hudson, NY: Anthroposophic Press, 1997).

CW 297 *Idee und Praxis der Waldorfschule (1919–1920)*. Dornach 1998. In English: *Rudolf Steiner in the Waldorf School* (Hudson, NY: Anthroposophic Press, 1996).

CW 297a *Erziehung zum Leben. Selbsterziehung und pädagogische Praxis (1921–1924)*. Dornach 1998.

CW 298 Rudolf Steiner in der Waldorfschule (1919–1924). Dornach 1980. In Englsih: *Rudolf Steiner in the Waldorf School* (Hudson, NY: Anthroposophic Press, 1996).

CW 301 *Die Erneuerung der pädagogisch-didaktischen Kunst durch Geisteswissenschaft (1920)*. Dornach 1991. In English: *The Renewal of Education* (Great Barrington, MA: SteinerBooks, 2002).

CW 302 *Menschenerkenntnis und Unterrichtsgestaltung (1921)*. Dornach 1986. In English: *Education for Adolescents* (Hudson, NY: Anthroposophic Press, 1996).

CW 302a *Erziehung und Unterricht aus Menschenerkenntnis (1920–1923)*. Dornach 1993. In English: *Balance in Teaching* (Great Barrington, MA: SteinerBooks, 2007).

Works Cited

CW 303 *Die gesunde Entwicklung des Menschenwesens. Eine Einführung in die anthroposophische Pädagogik und Didaktik (1921–1922).* Dornach 1987. In English: *Soul Economy: Body, Soul, and Spirit in Waldorf Education* (Great Barrington, MA: SteinerBooks, 2003).

CW 304 *Erziehungs- und Unterrichtsmethoden auf anthroposophischer Grundlage (1921–1922).* Dornach 1979. In English: *Waldorf Education and Anthroposophy 1* (Hudson, NY: Anthroposophic Press, 1995).

CW 304a *Anthroposophische Menschenkunde und Pädagogik (1923–1924).* Dornach 1979. In English: *Waldorf Education and Anthroposophy 2* (Hudson, NY: Anthroposophic Press, 1996).

CW 305 *Die geistig-seelischen Grundkräfte der Erziehungskunst. Spirituelle Werte in Erziehung und sozialem Leben (1922).* Dornach 1991. In English: *The Spiritual Ground of Education* (Great Barrington, MA: SteinerBooks, 2004).

CW 306 *Die pädagogische Praxis vom Gesichtspunkte geisteswissenschaftlicher Menschenerkenntnis. Die Erziehung des Kindes und jüngeren Menschen (1923).* Dornach 1989. In English: *The Child's Changing Consciousness* (Hudson, NY: Anthroposophic Press, 1996).

CW 307 *Gegenwärtiges Geistesleben und Erziehung (1923).* Dornach 1986. In English: *A Modern Art of Education* (Great Barrington, MA: Anthroposophic Press, 2004).

CW 308 *Die Methodik des Lehrens und die Lebensbedingungen des Erziehens (1924).* Dornach 1986. In English: *The Essentials of Education* (Hudson, NY: Anthroposophic Press, 1998).

CW 309 *Anthroposophische Pädagogik und ihre Voraussetzungen (1924).* Dornach 1981. In English: *The Roots of Education* (Hudson, NY: Anthroposophic Press, 1998).

CW 310 *Der pädagogische Wert der Menschenerkenntnis und der Kulturwert der Pädagogik (1924).* Dornach 1989. In English: *Human Values in Education* (Great Barrington, MA: SteinerBooks, 2002).

CW 311 *Die Kunst des Erziehens aus dem Erfassen der Menschenwesenheit (1924)*. Dornach 1989. In English: *The Kingdom of Childhood: Introductory Talks on Waldorf Education* (Hudson, NY: Anthroposophic Press, 1995).

CW 312 *Geisteswissenschaft und Medizin*. Dornach 1999. In English: *Introducing Anthroposophical Medicine* (Great Barrington, MA: SteinerBooks, 2010).

CW 314 *Physiologisch-Therapeutisches auf Grundlage der Geisteswissenschaft. Zur Therapie und Hygiene (1920–1924)*. Dornach 2010. In English: *Physiology and Healing: Treatment, Therapy, and Hygiene* (London: Rudolf Steiner Press, 2013).

CW 315 *Heileurythmie (1921–1922)*. Dornach 2003. In English: *Eurythmy Therapy* (London: Rudolf Steiner Press, 2009).

CW 316 *Meditative Betrachtungen und Anleitungen zur Vertiefung der Heilkunst. Vorträge für Ärzte und Medizinstudierende (1924)*. Dornach 2009. In English: *Understanding Healing: Meditative Reflections on Deepening Medicine through Spiritual Science* (London: Rudolf Steiner Press, 2013).

CW 317 *Heilpädagogischer Kurs (1924)*. Dornach 1995. In English: *Education for Special Needs: The Curative Education Course* (London: Rudolf Steiner Press, 2015).

CW 323 *Das Verhältnis der verschiedenen naturwissenschaftlichen Gebiete zur Astronomie. Dritter naturwissenschaftlicher Kurs: Himmelskunde in Beziehung zum Menschen und zur Menschenkunde (1921)*. Dornach 1997.

CW 330 *Neugestaltung des sozialen Organismus (1919)*. Dornach 1983.

Works Cited

By Other Authors

Bauer, Joachim. *Warum ich fühle, was du fühlst. Intuitive Kommunikation und das Geheimnis der Spiegelneurone.* München 2012.

Bowlby, John. *Bindung. Eine Analyse der Mutter-Kind-Beziehung.* München 1975.

———. *Trennung. Psychische Schäden als Folge der Trennung von Mutter und Kind.* Frankfurt a. M. 1994.

Dornes, Martin. *Der kompetente Säugling: die präverbale Entwicklung des Menschen.* Frankfurt 1993.

Fuchs, Thomas. *Leib, Raum, Person. Entwurf einer phänomenologischen Anthropologie.* Stuttgart 2000.

———. *Leib und Lebenswelt. Neun philosophisch-psychiatrische Essays.* Kusterdingen 2008a.

———. *Das Gehirn – ein Beziehungsorgan. Eine phänomenologisch-ökologische Konzeption.* Stuttgart 2008b.

Grossmann, Karin und Grossmann, Klaus E.. *Bindung und menschliche Entwicklung.* Stuttgart 2003.

König, Karl. *Die ersten drei Jahre des Kindes.* Stuttgart 1957.

———. *Sinnesentwicklung und Leiberfahrung.* Stuttgart 1971.

Kranich, Ernst-Michael. *Nachahmung als Grundform frühkindlichen Lernens.* In Leber, Stefan (ed.): *Die Pädagogik der Waldorfschule und ihre Grundlagen.* Darmstadt 1992.

———. *Anthropologische Grundlagen der Waldorfpädagogik.* Stuttgart 1999.

Leber, Stefan. *Die Menschenkunde der Waldorfpädagogik. Anthropologische Grundlagen der Erziehung des Kindes und Jugendlichen.* Stuttgart 1993.

———. *Kommentar zu Rudolf Steiners Vorträgen über «Allgemeine Menschenkunde als Grundlage der Pädagogin».* Band 1. Stuttgart 2002.

Montada, Leo (ed.). *Brennpunkte der Entwicklungspsychologie.* Stuttgart 1979.

Müller-Wiedemann, Hans. *Mitte der Kindheit. Das neunte bis zwölfte Lebensjahr. Beiträge zu einer anthroposophischen Entwicklungslehre.* Stuttgart 1989.

Neider, Andreas (ed.). *Lernen aus neurobiologischer, pädagogischer, entwicklungspychologischer und geisteswissenschaftlicher Sicht.* Stuttgart 2004.

Nitschke, Alfred. *Das verwaiste Kind der Natur.* Tübingen 1962.

Piaget, Jean. *Nachahmung, Spiel und Traum.* Stuttgart 1969.

———. *Das Weltbild des Kindes.* München 1978.

Prokofieff, Sergej O. *Und die Erde wird zur Sonne. Zum Mysterium der Auferstehung.* Arlesheim 2012.

———. *Die Begegnung mit dem Bösen und seine Überwindung in der Geisteswissenschaft. Der Grundstein des Guten.* Dornach 2015.

Rittelmeyer, Christian. *Pädagogische Anthropologie des Leibes. Biologische Voraussetzungen der Erziehung und Bildung.* Weinheim 2002.

———. *Frühe Erfahrungen des Kindes. Ergebnisse der pränatalen Psychologie und der Bindungsforschung. Ein Überblick.* Stuttgart 2005.

Schmelzer, Albert. *Die Dreigliederungs-Bewegung 1919. Rudolf Steiners Einsatz für den Selbstverwaltungsimpuls.* Stuttgart 1991.

Selg, Peter. *Krankheit und Christus-Erkenntnis, Anthroposophische Medizin als christliche Heilkunst.* Dornach 2001 [in English: *Seeing Christ in Sickness and Healing: Anthroposophical Medicine as a Medicine Founded in Christianity,* Floris Books 2005].

———. *Vom Logos menschlicher Physis. Die Entfaltung einer anthroposophischen Humanphysiologie im Werk Rudolf Steiners. Studienausgabe. Zwei Bände.* Dornach 2006.

———. *«Ich bin anders als Du». Vom Selbst- und Welterleben des Kindes in der Mitte der Kindheit.* Arlesheim 2011a [in English: *I Am Different from You: How Children Experience Themselves and the World in the Middle of Childhood.* SteinerBooks 2011.].

————. *Der geistige Kern der Waldorfschule.* Arlesheim 2011b [in English: *The Essence of Waldorf Education.* SteinerBooks 2010].

————. *Der therapeutische Blick. Rudolf Steiner sieht Kinder.* Dornach 2011c [in English: *The Therapeutic Eye: How Rudolf Steiner Observed Children.* SteinerBooks 2008].

————. *Rudolf Steiner. 1861–1925. Lebens- und Werkgeschichte. Drei Bände.* Arlesheim 2012a [in English: *Rudolf Steiner, Life and Work,* 7 vols. SteinerBooks 2014–].

————. *«Eine grandiose Metamorphose». Zur geisteswissenschaftlichen Anthropologie und Pädagogik des Jugendalters.* Dornach 2012b [in English: *A Grand Metamorphosis: Contributions to the Spiritual-Scientific Anthropology and Education of Adolescents.* SteinerBooks 2008].

————. *Ungeborenheit.* Arlesheim 2013 [in English: *Unbornness: Human Pre-existence and the Journey toward Birth.* SteinerBooks 2010].

————. *Anthroposophische Pädagogik.* Arlesheim 2015.

———— (ed.). *Rudolf Steiner. Texte zur Medizin. Teil 1: Physiologische Menschenkunde.* Dornach 2004.

———— (ed.). *Rudolf Steiner. Texte zur Medizin. Teil 2: Pathologie und Therapie.* Berlin 2014.

Spangler, Gottfried (ed.). *Die Bindungstheorie. Grundlagen, Forschung und Anwendung.* Stuttgart 1997.

Spitz, René. *Vom Säugling zum Kleinkind. Naturgeschichte der Mutter-Kind-Beziehungen im ersten Lebensjahr.* Stuttgart 1981.

Stern, Daniel. *Mutter und Kind–Die erste Beziehung.* Stuttgart 2000.

————. *Die Lebenserfahrungen des Säuglings.* Stuttgart 2003.

Tauler, Johannes. *Predigten.* Georg Hofmann (ed.). Band 1. Einsiedeln-Trier 1987.

Books in English Translation by Peter Selg

ON RUDOLF STEINER

Rudolf Steiner: Life and Work: (1914–1918): The Years of World War I , vol. 4 of 7 (2016)

Rudolf Steiner: Life and Work: (1900–1914): Spiritual Science and Spiritual Community, vol. 3 of 7 (2015)

Rudolf Steiner: Life and Work: (1890–1900): Weimar and Berlin, vol. 2 of 7 (2014)

Rudolf Steiner: Life and Work: (1861–1890): Childhood, Youth, and Study Years, vol. 1 of 7 (2014)

Rudolf Steiner and Christian Rosenkreutz (2012)

Rudolf Steiner as a Spiritual Teacher: From Recollections of Those Who Knew Him (2010)

CHRISTOLOGY

The Sufferings of the Nathan Soul: Anthroposophic Christology on the Eve of World War I (2016)

The Lord's Prayer and Rudolf Steiner: A Study of His Insights into the Archetypal Prayer of Christianity (2014)

The Creative Power of Anthroposophical Christology: An Outline of Occult Science · The First Goetheanum ·

The Fifth Gospel · The Christmas Conference (with Sergei O. Prokofieff) (2012)

Christ and the Disciples: *The Destiny of an Inner Community* (2012)

The Figure of Christ: *Rudolf Steiner and the Spiritual Intention behind the Goetheanum's Central Work of Art* (2009)

Rudolf Steiner and the Fifth Gospel: *Insights into a New Understanding of the Christ Mystery* (2010)

Seeing Christ in Sickness and Healing (2005)

GENERAL ANTHROPOSOPHY

The Michael School: *And the School of Spiritual Science* (2016)

The Destiny of the Michael Community: *Foundation Stone for the Future* (2014)

Spiritual Resistance: *Ita Wegman 1933–1935* (2014)

The Last Three Years: *Ita Wegman in Ascona, 1940–1943* (2014)

From Gurs to Auschwitz: *The Inner Journey of Maria Krehbiel-Darmstädter* (2013)

Crisis in the Anthroposophical Society: *And Pathways to the Future* (2013); with Sergei O. Prokofieff

Rudolf Steiner's Foundation Stone Meditation: *And the Destruction of the Twentieth Century* (2013)

The Culture of Selflessness: Rudolf Steiner, the Fifth Gospel, and the Time of Extremes (2012)

The Mystery of the Heart: The Sacramental Physiology of the Heart in Aristotle, Thomas Aquinas, and Rudolf Steiner (2012)

Rudolf Steiner and the School for Spiritual Science: The Foundation of the "First Class" (2012)

Rudolf Steiner's Intentions for the Anthroposophical Society: The Executive Council, the School for Spiritual Science, and the Sections (2011)

The Fundamental Social Law: Rudolf Steiner on the Work of the Individual and the Spirit of Community (2011)

The Path of the Soul after Death: The Community of the Living and the Dead as Witnessed by Rudolf Steiner in his Eulogies and Farewell Addresses (2011)

The Agriculture Course, Koberwitz, Whitsun 1924: Rudolf Steiner and the Beginnings of Biodynamics (2010)

ANTHROPOSOPHICAL MEDICINE AND CURATIVE EDUCATION

The Warmth Meditation: A Path to the Good in the Service of Healing (2016)

Honoring Life: Medical Ethics and Physician-Assisted Suicide (2014); with Sergei O. Prokofieff

I Am for Going Ahead: Ita Wegman's Work for the Social Ideals of Anthroposophy (2012)

The Child with Special Needs: Letters and Essays on Curative Education (Ed.) (2009)

Ita Wegman and Karl König: Letters and Documents (2008)

Karl König's Path to Anthroposophy (2008)

Karl König: My Task: Autobiography and Biographies (Ed.) (2008)

CHILD DEVELOPMENT AND WALDORF EDUCATION

The Child as a Sense Organ: An Anthroposophic Understanding of the Imitation Processes (2017)

I Am Different from You: How Children Experience Themselves and the World in the Middle of Childhood (2011)

Unbornness: Human Pre-existence and the Journey toward Birth (2010)

The Essence of Waldorf Education (2010)

The Therapeutic Eye: How Rudolf Steiner Observed Children (2008)

A Grand Metamorphosis: Contributions to the Spiritual-Scientific Anthropology and Education of Adolescents (2008)

Ita Wegman Institute
for Basic Research into Anthroposophy

Pfeffinger Weg 1a, ch 4144 Arlesheim, Switzerland
www.wegmaninstitut.ch
e-mail: sekretariat@wegmaninstitut.ch

The Ita Wegman Institute for Basic Research into Anthroposophy is a non-profit research and teaching organization. It undertakes basic research into the lifework of Dr. Rudolf Steiner (1861–1925) and the application of Anthroposophy in specific areas of life, especially medicine, education, and curative education. Work carried out by the Institute is supported by a number of foundations and organizations and an international group of friends and supporters. The Director of the Institute is Prof. Dr. Peter Selg.